# THE OSAGE IN MISSOURI

T0170833

**Project Sponsors**
Missouri Center for the Book
Western Historical Manuscript Collection, University of
Missouri–Columbia

**Special Thanks**
A. E. Schroeder
Paul Szopa, Academic Support Center, University of
Missouri–Columbia
Missouri Department of Natural Resources
State Historical Society of Missouri, Columbia

## Missouri Heritage Readers

*General Editor,*
REBECCA B. SCHROEDER

Each Missouri Heritage Reader explores a particular aspect of the state's rich cultural heritage. Focusing on people, places, historical events, and the details of daily life, these books illustrate the ways in which people from all parts of the world contributed to the development of the state and the region. The books incorporate documentary and oral history, folklore, and informal literature in a way that makes these resources accessible to all Missourians.

Intended primarily for adult new readers, these books will also be invaluable to readers of all ages interested in the cultural and social history of Missouri.

**Books in the Series**

# THE OSAGE IN MISSOURI

## Kristie C. Wolferman

University of Missouri Press
Columbia and London

Library of Congress Cataloging-in-Publication Data

Wolferman, Kristie C., 1948–
    The Osage in Missouri / Kristie C. Wolferman.
        p.   cm.—(Missouri heritage readers)
    Includes bibliographical references and index.
    ISBN 0-8262-1122-4 (pbk. : alk. paper)
    1. Osage Indians—History—Juvenile literature.   2. Osage
  Indians—Social life and customes—Juvenile literature.   I. Title.
  II. Series.
  E99.08W65   1997
  973'.049752—dc21                                           97-10975
                                                                CIP


∞™ This paper meets the requirements of the
American National Standard for Permanence of Paper
for Printed Library Materials, Z39.48, 1984.

Designer: Stephanie Foley
Typesetter: BOOKCOMP
Printer and Binder: Thomson-Shore, Inc.
Typeface: Palatino and Saddlebag

*To my students,*
*who kept asking questions to which*
*we could not find the answers,*
*and to my family for its support.*

# Contents

# Acknowledgments

I am grateful to institutions and individuals who helped me find information and illustrations for this book, including the Jackson County Historical Society, Lindenwood College, Fort Osage, the Nelson-Atkins Museum of Art, the Missouri Historical Society, and the Native Sons Collection. Special thanks go to David Boutros at the Western Historical Manuscript Collection in Kansas City, to Fae Sotham at the State Historical Society of Missouri in Columbia, and to Sally Schilling, Government Documents Librarian, Ellis Library, University of Missouri, Columbia.

I would also like to thank Dean Michael O'Brien for his readings of the manuscript and his many helpful suggestions.

# THE OSAGE IN MISSOURI

# Introduction

On November 10, 1808, a cannon boom announced the opening of Fort Osage. The new fort was perched on a bluff overlooking the Missouri River about 250 miles west of St. Louis. The American militia and the chiefs from the Little Osage and Big Osage nations celebrated. On that date the Indians and white men signed a treaty, written by Meriwether Lewis, governor of the Louisiana Territory, and passed a peace pipe to demonstrate their friendship.

In Washington, too, the christening of Fort Osage seemed cause for celebration. The fort was the first of twenty-eight fort–trading posts the U.S. government planned to build in the Louisiana Territory. President Thomas Jefferson hoped that Fort Osage and the fort–trading post concept would not only open the West to white settlement but also begin a new era in relations between the United States and Native Americans.

On their historic exploration of the Louisiana Territory, Meriwether Lewis and William Clark had chosen the site for Fort Osage in 1804. The site met the plan set forth by President Jefferson. Its strategic position on the river would make the fort defensible; its accessibility to Indian tribes would make it suitable as a trading post. By opening the fort, Jefferson could achieve his dual aims of westward expansion and fair trade with the Indian tribes.

For a short time, the fort would provide the dominant tribe in the area, the Osage, with a place to trade their furs for the European goods they sought. It would also offer them some protection from other tribes. However, the Osage chiefs

1

In this portrait by Charles Bird King, Mo-Hon-Go, an Osage woman, and her child are dressed in cotton clothing but wear traditional decorative jewelry. The baby is wearing a presidential peace medal. (State Historical Society of Missouri, Columbia.)

found out very quickly that they had given up more than they had gained by signing the Fort Osage treaty. In spite of the good intentions of Jefferson and his ambassadors, the Fort Osage experiment came too late to help establish good relations between white settlers and the native population.

The traders and soldiers at the fort–trading house were not the first white men the Osage had seen. Trappers, traders, and missionaries had come before the militia; more missionaries, as well as settlers, were at their heels. The same pattern of encounters between Europeans and natives that had been going on for more than two hundred years in North America would be repeated in the West. The newcomers would settle Osage land; and Osage culture, already greatly altered by Europeans and Americans, would never be the same again.

# 1

# Missouri's First Inhabitants

Of all the Indians living within Missouri during historic times, none excited the interest or the admiration
of the whites more than the Osage.

—CHARLES VAN RAVENSWAAY,
*Missouri: A Guide to the Show-me State*

By the time Fort Osage opened in 1808, there were many
tribes of Indians settled in what would become the state
of Missouri. The major tribe of the area was the Osage.
However, the Kaskaskia, an Illinois tribe, had lived in northeastern Missouri from time to time; the Iowa tribe had occupied the northwestern part of the state. Shortly before 1800,
Delaware and Shawnee tribes moved from their northeastern
and Ohio Valley homesites to eastern Missouri, setting up
camps in the foothills of the Ozarks and in the Mississippi
Valley. Cherokees, moving from their southeastern homeland,
settled along the St. Francis River in southeastern Missouri and
northeastern Arkansas prior to the Louisiana Purchase. Other
displaced eastern and southeastern tribes, including the Sauk,
Fox, Miami, Kickapoo, and Wea tribes, lived in the state for
short periods. (Most of the Missouri tribe, for whom the state

would be named, had joined other tribes by the late eighteenth century.) The waterway system of Missouri allowed easy contact with neighbors, and the traditional, historic culture of the Osage tribe had been influenced and disrupted by other tribes and by white trappers and traders long before Fort Osage was established.

Even before their encounter with displaced tribes, the Osage Indians had adopted many of the traits of eastern, southeastern, and plains Indians. The best way to describe the Osage Indians' way of life is that it was a prairie culture, different from the woodlands, plains, or southeastern tribes that surrounded the area.

Located as they were in the center of the continent, Missouri natives were in an area where different geographies and cultures met and blended together. Physically, what is now the state of Missouri consists of river lowlands in the southeast, the Ozark highland in the south-central area, and prairies in the west reaching toward the Great Plains. From the eastern woodlands to the western grasslands, there is a marked change. The diversity of plant and animal life in these different habitats shaped the customs of the native peoples, allowing them a wide variety of choices to meet their basic needs. The land was so rich in natural resources that in 1717 a young Frenchman, Etienne de Véniard, sieur de Bourgmont, described the area as "the finest country and the most beautiful land in the world; the prairies are like the seas and filled with wild animals; especially oxen, cattle, hind and stag, in such quantities as to surpass the imagination."

Missouri also is at the heart of the North American waterway system, allowing river transportation in any direction. The rivers served as channels to carry ideas as well as trade items. Long before the Osage had become a distinct and separate tribe (which may not have been until around 1500), natives in Missouri established a river-based culture that was greatly influenced by trade with other tribal groups.

More than a thousand years ago, a great mound center arose at Cahokia, near what is now St. Louis. This site was located on

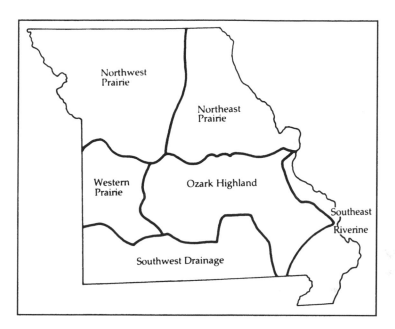

The geography of Missouri varies widely from the southeastern river lowlands to the Ozark highlands in the central area and on to the prairies in the west. (From Carl H. and Eleanor F. Chapman, *Indians and Archaeology of Missouri.*)

the east bank of the Mississippi River. The people who lived there, called the Mississippians, depended on the river for fish and used the river bottomlands to grow a variety of crops. Although the mound city at Cahokia was a major center of population, other Mississippians lived in surrounding areas. These village farmers inhabited wood-framed houses with thatched roofs. Their homes were usually grouped in towns, each town with its own temple mound. Like the Cahokians, the village farmers depended on the resources of the waterways.

During the time Cahokia thrived (in an era now called the Mississippi Period), there was a continuous stream of people coming and going on the rivers. People in outlying communities went to Cahokia in dugout canoes to barter goods and exchange presents and ideas. Salt, obtained from salt springs not far from Cahokia, was a major trade item, as was pottery, manufactured by the village women. Skilled craftsmen carved bone, antler, shell, and stone. Copper was a sacred material, of great value and esteem, highly desired by Cahokians.

The Cahokian culture was at its peak around A.D. 1000–1200. In about A.D. 1350 another fully developed culture, the Oneota, appeared around the mouth of the Grand River in central Missouri. Although the Oneota lived in permanent villages, they sent hunting parties west to the plains to hunt buffalo and other big game. They were much less dependent on river trade than were the Cahokians, and they did not have temple mounds. Like the village farmers, however, they did tend crops, produce pottery, and fish the rivers.

In 1541, when Hernando de Soto crossed the Mississippi River into present-day Arkansas, the great mound center at Cahokia had long since been vacated. The Mississippian culture, however, was still thriving in northeastern Arkansas and throughout the Southeast. Some historians blame de Soto for the rapid decline of the village farmers in the years after his visit. De Soto's cruel army looted and destroyed villages, causing chaos in the natives' carefully balanced town structure. De Soto's march also had a long-lasting effect on all existing settlements by introducing European diseases to the native peoples. The Native Americans had little resistance to or experience with contagious disease, and large numbers of them died.

Most archaeologists believe that the Missouri, and probably the Osage, stemmed from the Oneota culture. Many other theories exist about the origins of the Osage. Nineteenth-century ethnologist James Owen Dorsey accepted the Osage belief that the Osage people originally inhabited the Ohio Valley along with other Dhegiha Siouan–speaking tribes, including the Kansas, Poncas, Quapaws, and Omahas. Other authorities say the Osage originated in the southeastern part of the United States. Another theory is that the Osage and other Siouan tribes, including the Missouri, came from the north.

The debate about the origin of the Osage may never be resolved. Their seminomadic habits make their history difficult to trace. There is little archaeological evidence of the

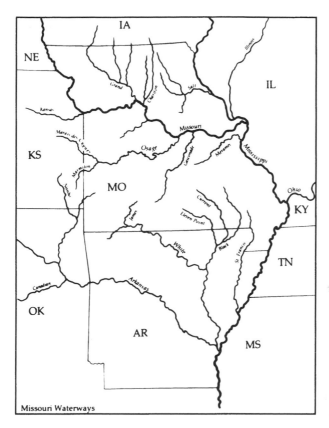

IA
NE
IL
KS
MO
KY
TN
OK
AR
MS

Missouri Waterways

Missouri's geographic location, at the heart of North America's waterway system, allowed exchange of ideas and goods. (From Carl H. and Eleanor F. Chapman, *Indians and Archaeology of Missouri.*)

Osage dating before 1700; there are no written accounts before European contact with them. The French and Spanish traders, the first Europeans in the Missouri Valley, left some records of their dealings with the Osage. However, they did not attempt to learn very much about the natives' culture. When later ethnologists interviewed Osage elders to try to understand Osage traditions and ways of life, the Osage were settled on reservations. Much of their culture had changed; some of their history had been forgotten during the preceding two hundred years of European contact.

# 2

# The Osage Traditions

Deer, wild turkey, and other game abounded in the primeval forest, the beautiful Osage river and its tributaries were full of fish, and in less than a day's journey were the great prairies where large herds of buffalo roamed. . . . What more could they ask?

—MRS. W. W. GRAVES,
"In the Land of the Osages . . .",
*Missouri Historical Review*, February 1924

The Osage were among the most important of the Dhegiha Siouan tribes. They were certainly the most numerous tribe in Missouri at one time. According to an estimate reported by historian John R. Swanton, the Osage population was sixty-two hundred in 1780.

Early in their history, the Osage divided into two groups. A natural disaster was the supposed cause for the split. Many, many years before, according to legend, the Osage people were camped along a river (it could have been any of several rivers associated with Osage history). Torrential rains began to fall. As the rains continued day after day, the river began to flood the Osage camps, and the Osage were forced to flee. They left

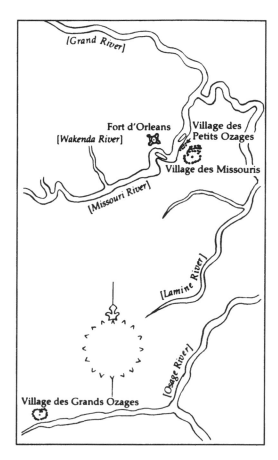

A map drawn sometime between 1723 and 1728 shows that the Little Osage had broken away from the Big Osage and formed a separate village near the Missouri tribe. (From Carl H. and Eleanor F. Chapman, *Indians and Archaeology of Missouri.*)

in five groups. One group climbed the bluffs by the river and went into the woods beyond the bluffs; some even climbed trees. These people were called "Top-of-the-Tree Sitters." Another group stopped on the bluffs and built fires to dry their belongings. They were called "Upper-Forest Sitters." A third group ran up the valley of the feeder stream where water locusts grew in abundance. Thus, they were named "Sitters-in-the-Locusts." Another group stayed in the flooded village, hanging onto anything that floated. They became known as the "Heart-Stays People." A fifth group fled the flooded village but stopped under the bluffs and waited for the floodwater to recede. They were described as "Down-Below People."

Sometime after the flood, the five groups became two: the "Upper-Forest Sitters" and the "Down-Below People." It became customary for the Down-Below People to camp below the Upper-Forest Sitters. Much later, through a French missionary's misinterpretation of sign language, the Down-Below People came to be called the Little Osage, and the Upper-Forest Sitters were called the Great or Big Osage.

The Little Osage continued to camp below the Big Osage until around 1720, when the Little Osage actually left the Big Osage and moved to a separate village. In 1714, Etienne de Véniard, sieur de Bourgmont had visited the tribes; according to archaeologist Carl Chapman, he had encouraged the Little Osage to set up their own camp. Bourgmont offered the Little Osage trading opportunities once they broke away from the Big Osage. A map drawn between 1723 and 1728 shows separate villages. The Big Osage lived on the Osage River, and the Little Osage settled on the Missouri River near the Missouri Indians.

Some Osage began to settle in Arkansas in the 1770s, and shortly after 1800, a group left the Big Osage and moved to the Arkansas River. They became known as the Arkansas Band of the Osage.

The Osage traditionally called themselves "Ni-U-Ko'n-Ska," "Children of the Middle Waters." Of their own origin the Osage had no doubt. They knew that they came from the sky, where they had been children of Grandfather Sun. They fell to the earth in three groups. The People of the Water led. Then came the People of the Land; and finally, the People of the Sky. The Earth and Sky People divided into clans and came to dwell in an area where many forks of the Osage River meet. The French named one of those river forks the Marais des Cygnes, the Marsh of the Swans, a rough translation of the Osage name for their homeland. It was here that the early Osage villages were located.

The Osage village was carefully organized in a camp circle, with each clan arranged by its rank in the tribe. The chief's house was inside the circle and was somewhat larger than

The Osage village was arranged in a circle, with the Osage chief's house, which was slightly larger than the others, on the inside of the circle. (Osage Village State Historic Site, Missouri Department of Natural Resources.)

the other houses. The Osage homes were rectangular, oval, or sometimes circular. They were at least fifteen feet wide and varied from thirty to more than forty-five feet in length. They were built with center posts, eight feet apart, supporting a ridgepole. Attached to the ridge were bent poles that formed the roof. Anchored into the ground and fastened to the roof were wall posts that were at least five feet in height with crossbars at right angles. Overlapping woven mats, or sometimes buffalo hides, covered this arborlike frame. Each house had one or more fireplaces with smoke holes in the roof. The only other opening in the Osage house was a doorway on the long side. It faced the east, so that as they left the house in the morning, the Osage could say their early prayers facing the rising sun.

Just as the Osage village was organized in a certain manner, every aspect of the Osage way of life was strictly regulated

Osage men were usually more than six feet tall. They wore their hair in a roach style and dressed in loincloths, moccasins, and leggings. (From George Catlin, *North American Indians,* State Historical Society of Missouri, Columbia.)

by tribal custom. A select group of elder warriors, known as the Little Old Men, served as the keepers of tradition. They set the standards of conduct and were the actual governing body of the tribe. Each Osage village had one or two chiefs, who were leaders rather than rulers. Chiefs inherited their positions from their fathers, but they had limited power. The Little Old Men could remove them from authority if they proved to be unworthy.

Many explorers and travelers considered the Osage to be a very handsome people. Washington Irving, who traveled around the country and met many native tribes, said the Osage were "the finest looking Indians in the West." The men were very tall, usually six feet or more, and very well proportioned. They wore their hair in a roach style, shaving their eyebrows, face, and head except for a scalp lock about two inches high and three inches wide that ran down the back of their heads to the nape of their necks. Because of their repugnance for hair, the first encounter the Osages had with the French was a shock

Every morning Osage women and girls painted the parts in their hair red to allow them to face each day bravely. (From Carl H. and Eleanor F. Chapman, *Indians and Archaeology of Missouri.*)

to them. They called the French "I'n-shta-heh," or "Heavy Eyebrows," and this was not a compliment.

Osage women wore their long hair loosely flowing down their backs. They powdered their bodies with a dark substance that came from a beanlike flowering plant and wore pumpkin pulp on their faces to improve their complexions. Perhaps for these reasons, Europeans found the Osage women to be less attractive than the men.

Osage children, who were very much coddled and adored, also appeared quite strange to Europeans. Babies were placed on cradleboards, boards about three feet long and about one foot wide with square ends. The children's heads became flattened from resting against the back of the cradleboard, a physical feature that the Osage found attractive.

Osage men dressed in loincloths, moccasins, and leggings made of deerskin or bearskin. They wore buffalo robes to

Both men and women decorated their bodies with tattoos, using tattoo sticks to etch the designs. (From *Smithsonian Miscellaneous Collections*, vol. 63, 1914.)

keep warm in the winter. They wore ear ornaments, bracelets, and tattoos on their chests and arms. The women dressed in deerskin robes, moccasins, and leggings. They belted their dresses with woven buffalo calves' hair or, after the Europeans began trading with them, with brightly colored woolen belts. Like the men, the women liked jewelry and wore earrings and bracelets. They also decorated themselves with elaborate tattoos. Each morning the women and girls painted the parts in their hair red. This custom was to symbolize the path of the sun across the sky. They believed the red paint would grant them a long life and allow them to face each day bravely.

Men and women had specific jobs, and the children learned from their elders. In general, the men hunted for game and went to war. The women built houses, tended children, manufactured important household items, made clothes, gathered edible plants, and gardened. Women made pottery and an assortment of wooden tools and containers. They used flint, bone, or antler for awls, needles, scrapers, and other implements. After the Osage began to trade with the Europeans, however, trade goods made of iron, copper, and brass replaced the items the Osage women had made.

The food that women and children gathered included persimmons, nuts, and water lily roots. The gardens for each village adjoined one another outside the circle of houses. Each family had a garden that was at most half an acre. The women planted corn, beans, and squash in April. They cultivated the plants once in May and then left the fields alone until August harvest time. From May through July, almost everyone left the villages to hunt for bear, buffalo, and deer. Only a few elders remained behind to tend the gardens. Again in the fall, the men hunted for buffalo and deer from early September until December. After the European fur trade became important, beaver became a prime fall hunting target. On their hunts, the Osage lived in cone-shaped portable wigwams or tepee-style houses of buffalo skin.

The Osage had the reputation of being a warlike tribe. Warfare dominated Osage life, and all Osage men wanted to become warriors. Men strived to earn honor, or what the French called "coup," through their daring. Stealing horses and killing enemies were honored acts, but touching an enemy was the bravest deed possible. To touch an enemy alive or just after he died would earn a warrior a "coup" feather. Osage warfare consisted of lightning-fast raids. Their purpose was to kill or injure the enemy and to steal horses and other goods.

The Osage used bows and arrows, lances, wooden clubs, tomahawks, and knives as weapons. They made their bows and quivers from a flexible wood, such as ash. After the French made contact with the Osage in the late seventeenth century, the Osage acquired European weapons. They employed muskets, sabers, iron knives, and tomahawks. They still used bows and arrows to hunt, but now they preferred arrowheads made of brass, copper, or iron. When the Spanish introduced horses, the Osage way of hunting changed forever. The Osage

Shon-Ge-Mon-In counts
his war honors. (*Thirty-Ninth
Annual Report of the Bureau of
American Ethnology, 1917–1918,*
1925. Courtesy Smithsonian
Institution.)

obtained horses through trade or raids on plains or Southwest
tribes. Having horses gave them more mobility both to hunt
and to fight.

The Osage had many opportunities to fight. During the
eighteenth century practically everyone was the enemy of the
Osage. They were at war with all the plains tribes and many of
the woodlands tribes as well. This was a difficult situation for
the Europeans to understand. They did not appreciate how
important honor in war was to the Osage. Osage warriors
believed that death in battle was the most honorable way to
die. They believed that those who were killed fighting would

spend their afterlives in a village that had plenty of horses and wild game. However, if they died of an illness or from some other cause, they would reside forever in a poor village with little to recommend it.

Tradition, family, and ceremony were of great importance to the Osage. Their lives followed familiar cycles of nature, which were governed by the spirit that made them all, Wah'Kon-Tah. The Osage rituals celebrated the balance of nature and the myths of creation.

When white men intruded into their world, the Osage way of life changed dramatically.

# 3

# The French and the Fur Trade

Spanish civilization crushed the Indian; English civilization scorned and neglected him; French civilization embraced and cherished him.

—FRANCIS PARKMAN,
nineteenth-century historian

Of the Missouri Native American tribes, neither the Osage nor the Missouri had ever lived in isolation from their neighbors. They traveled to hunt, to trade, to raid, and to fight other tribes. Before European explorers, traders, or missionaries found them in Missouri, it is likely that Missouri tribes had made contact with Europeans elsewhere.

The first documented case of white men venturing into Osage and Missouri territory occurred in 1673. Father Jacques Marquette and Louis Jolliet left St. Ignace, a remote Ottawa mission Marquette had established near the Straits of Mackinac in present-day Michigan. They traveled down the Mississippi River to the Arkansas River. On their way, they "discovered" the Pekitanoui, or Missouri, River.

Near the end of June 1673, Marquette and Jolliet became the first known white men to see and note the mouth of the

Missouri. From their Ottawa guides they had heard stories of the great Pekitanoui, located some six or seven days' journey down the Mississippi River from the junction of the Mississippi with the Illinois River. They had also heard that the Pekitanoui flowed west, possibly to the sea. Perhaps it would be the shortcut to Asia that every explorer since Christopher Columbus had looked for.

Although Marquette and Jolliet knew nothing firsthand about the native inhabitants, the Ottawa Indians had told them about the "prodigious nations, who use wooden canoes and who made the Missouri River region their home." Excited about finding the Missouri, the explorers claimed the area for France and declared all its inhabitants to be subjects of the French crown.

Both Marquette and Jolliet drew maps of the Missouri River Valley. The map that Marquette drew (incorrectly) showed a large, short river, ending abruptly. Little did he know that the Missouri River was the largest branch of the longest river in North America. However, he was able to locate correctly several tribes dwelling on the river, including the Ouchage (Osage), Ouemessourit (Missouri), Kansa, and Paniassa (Pawnee).

Another French expedition, coming from Canada, reached the Missouri River on February 14, 1682. This group of twenty-three Frenchmen and thirty-one Indians was headed by René-Robert Cavelier, sieur de La Salle. Traveling in the dead of winter, La Salle's expedition journeyed through the Straits of Mackinac, down the east coast of Lake Michigan, and up the Chicago River to the Mississippi River, where ice delayed travel for about a week. When La Salle and his group reached the "grand rivière des Émisourites," they camped on the west bank of the Mississippi near the Missouri River's mouth. La Salle estimated that the Missouri was navigable for four hundred leagues or more: He believed it took a southwestwardly course to the mines of New Mexico and then on to the ocean. La Salle thought finding a route to the Spanish trading

Father Jacques Marquette descended the Mississippi River with Louis Jolliet. They were the first white men to note the mouth of the Peki-tanoui, or Missouri, River. (From William H. Milburn, *The Lance, Cross, and Canoe*, 1892, State Historical Society of Missouri, Columbia.)

area and the western sea would be very desirable. Therefore, when he completed his trip to the mouth of the Mississippi, he claimed the entire Mississippi Valley for France, naming it Louisiana in honor of his king, Louis XIV.

La Salle and his company also learned something about the people who lived along the Missouri River. Father Zenobe Membre, the chaplain and record keeper for the expedition, noted, "A great number of large villages, of many different nations" existed on this river. The people traveled by canoe. They hunted, for there was an abundance of bison and beaver that made their homes in this prairie land. Given the European fancy for beaver hats, the knowledge that the Missouri River area had many beaver became a major factor in drawing French traders and trappers.

During the 1690s, several French traders made contact with the natives who lived along the Missouri River. The first people the trappers found were a powerful and numerous group who camped near the river's mouth. These Indians called themselves the Mintache, meaning "those who reached the mouth of the river." However, their name for the great river was the Missouri, which in their language meant either "(people having) dugout canoes" or "(people having) wooden canoes." Through a misunderstanding, the river's name was interpreted to mean "Great Mud." This was an appropriate name for the muddy and snag-ridden river, whose nickname even today is "Big Muddy." The French used the Indian name for the Missouri River, but they also called the Mintache the "Missouri," because the Mintache were the first Indians they had seen on the Missouri River. Thus, the Missouri tribe acquired an importance far out of proportion to its size. Eventually, not only the river and the tribe but also several towns, the territory, the valley, and then the state would be called Missouri.

In May 1693, two French traders and some Kaskaskia Indians visited the Missouri and the Osage with the purpose of making an alliance and opening a trading relationship. These French trader-trappers were some of the first coureurs de bois, or woods rangers, in the Missouri Valley region. They established friendly relations with the Indians, learned their language, and started what would be a successful business venture. The coureurs de bois led a very unsettled life, traveling and bargaining, trading and risking their own personal safety to make a profit for their financial backers. When the Jesuits opened a mission at Cahokia in 1699, they expressed their disapproval of the "scandalous and criminal life" of the coureurs de bois. Nonetheless, a French settlement grew near the Cahokia mission and served as a starting point and business center for trading expeditions.

From 1700 on, there were many reports of explorations and trading trips up the Missouri River. By 1704, more than a hundred Frenchmen, working in groups of seven or eight, plied the Missouri River. They traveled in canoes or pirogues, hollowed-out wooden boats, adopted from the Indians. They

A French trapper, or coureur de bois, travels a Missouri waterway by canoe to trade European-manufactured goods to the Indians for furs. (State Historical Society of Missouri, Columbia.)

bargained with the natives for furs in exchange for European-manufactured trade goods.

In 1713, Bourgmont surveyed the Missouri River as far as the Platte River, mapping the area with incredible detail and accuracy. He became friendly with the Missouri and the Little Osage and wrote an account of the native people:

> There are the Missouris, a nation of savages, bearing the name of the river, who are allies of the French. There are also the Auzages [Osages], another savage nation, allies and friends of the French. Their entire commerce is in furs; they are not numerous; they are a splendid race, and more alert than any other nation. . . . They hunt almost entirely with the arrow; they have splendid horses and are fine riders.

Another Frenchman, Claude-Charles DuTisné, was the first official visitor to the Osage. In the spring of 1719 he set out from Kaskaskia, Illinois, on the Mississippi. He planned to explore

**FORT ORLEANS**
(Continued from other side)

Westernmost outpost of France in what is now Missouri, the establishment at Fort Orleans included a chapel, first Catholic church in the Missouri Valley. The first resident priest was Abbé Mercier.

When the fort was built, De Bourgmond traveled into what is now central Kansas, 1724, where he fulfilled his commission to make peace with the Comanches. In 1725 he returned to France taking several Indian chiefs and a young Missouri maiden along for a visit. The whole party delighted the French who called the girl "Princess of the Missouri," saw her baptized in Notre Dame, and married to a sergeant. De Bourgmond was made a noble and had for his coat of arms an Indian against a silver mountain.

De Bourgmond stayed in France, and in 1728 the fort was closed. Fort Orleans was built in territory claimed for France, 1682, and named Louisiana after Louis XIV by La Salle. France held the greater part of this claim 80 years, then ceded it, 1762, to Spain which held it 38 years, returning it to France, 1800, which sold it to the United States, 1803.

Erected by State Historical Society of Missouri
and State Highway Commission, 1953

In 1723, Etienne de Véniard, sieur de Bourgmont supervised the construction of the first Missouri post, Fort Orleans. A marker is located near Brunswick in Chariton County. (Photograph by A. E. Schroeder.)

the Missouri River and make treaties with the Osage, Paniouassa (Black Pawnee), and Padoucas (plains Apaches). First, DuTisné visited the Big Osage. They treated him hospitably and traded with him. However, when DuTisné announced that he planned to continue his trip southwest to the Black Pawnees and then to the Apaches, the Osage discouraged him from going on. They did not want him to visit their enemies, especially the hated Apaches, because they feared DuTisné wanted to trade guns to them. When DuTisné insisted on continuing his trip, the Osage forced him to leave all his trade goods with them. They grudgingly provided the Frenchman with a few horses and a guide-interpreter to go as far as the

Black Pawnee village. But the Osage sent messengers ahead to the Black Pawnees with false information about DuTisné's mission. The Osage messengers told the Black Pawnees that DuTisné and his men wanted to enslave some Black Pawnees.

When DuTisné arrived at the Black Pawnees' village, they were not friendly. However, because he was very bold, a quality much admired, DuTisné was able to gain the trust of the Black Pawnees and make a trade agreement with them. He also promised them that he would not go on to the land of the Apaches but would instead return to the Osage village. There, DuTisné retrieved his trade goods, but the Osage wanted nothing more to do with him. They refused to give him guides to help him return to Kaskaskia, so he had to finish his journey with only a compass to help him.

Even though DuTisné was the first European to make a recorded visit to the Osage, his report shows that before his contact with them, the Osage way of life had already been changed by Europeans. The Osage had horses, which presumably they had obtained indirectly or directly from the Spanish. Artifacts from the Utz site, the earliest known Osage camp in central Missouri, show that by 1700, nineteen years before DuTisné's visit, the Osage had acquired many European trade goods. Archaeologists found glass bottles, glass beads, and European-made ornaments. Other artifacts predating 1700 included European iron scraping and digging tools, trinkets, cloth goods, iron arrowheads, and guns. The arts of flint-knapping and pottery-making lost importance when European-made brass kettles replaced Osage pottery. The Osage were very quick to adopt European trade goods. And, because they knew how much the traders wanted their furs, they also became more demanding about the goods they took in trade.

For their part, the Europeans counted on the Osage to supply them with the fur pelts they needed. From 1700 on, a tremendous amount of commerce was built up between the Native Americans and the Europeans, based entirely on the fur trade. St. Louis became the headquarters for this business, which necessarily involved investing, provisioning, warehousing, financing, and accommodating more and more sophisticated tribal tastes. Although complete trading statistics are not available, we know that in 1757 about one hundred packs of mostly beaver skins were sent down the Missouri River from Kawsmouth alone. Between 1790 and 1804, fur trade from the Missouri River region at St. Louis amounted to more than two hundred thousand dollars. This was big business, a business that continued regardless of who owned the Louisiana Territory.

From 1682, when La Salle claimed the Louisiana region for France, until after the Treaty of Paris was signed in 1763, the French governed the Missouri River Valley. The most obvious aspect of government involvement was in the form of trading rights. The right to conduct trade with the Indians was granted to a few individuals or congés. Those with congé privileges were given territories, which could be major posts, regions, or rivers. In turn, the congés granted licenses to voyageurs who acquired trade goods and boats. The voyageurs then hired engagés who signed up for terms—usually three years—to go and trade directly with the Indians. These traders had to know what goods would sell to which tribes, had to know the best beaver pelt season (late fall), had to be diplomatic, and had to be excellent salesmen.

Apart from trading, the French established their presence in the Mississippi and Missouri Valleys by settling there. The earliest French city west of the Mississippi in Upper Louisiana was Ste. Geneviève. The French government also established a few military posts or forts. The purpose of these forts was to keep the voyageurs and coureurs de bois under control and to manage the fur trade, making sure that only licensed traders dealt with the Indians.

The first Missouri post was built by Bourgmont. In 1723 he erected a classic French colonial frontier fort on the north side of the Missouri River across from the Missouri Indian village. The fort was near present-day Brunswick, Missouri. Bourgmont named the small row of stockade buildings Fort

Orleans after the French regent then in power, the Duke of
Orléans. The fort became a meeting point for Indians and
traders alike.

It was at this post in 1724 that Bourgmont gathered a group
of Indians and French soldiers to explore farther west. Bourgmont's goal was to conduct a peace-seeking expedition to visit
the Apaches, who were the feared and hated enemies of the
Osage. Nomadic plains dwellers, the Apaches attacked any
intruders on their hunting grounds. When the Osage took their
buffalo hunting trips to the plains, they were often victims of
the Apaches. If attacked, the Osage, of course, retaliated. They
raided Apache camps, sometimes taking captives to sell as
slaves and often capturing horses and stealing other items.
The Apaches traded with the Spanish at Santa Fe, so they had
a wealth of trade goods and horses that were of interest to the
Osage. The French knew, and the Osage had been persuaded,
that it would benefit them to establish a friendly relationship
with the Apaches in order to gain trading rights in Santa Fe.

On June 25, 1724, Bourgmont left Fort Orleans with eleven
soldiers, one hundred Missouri Indians, and sixty-four Osages
led by four war chiefs. They stopped at the Kansa village
on the Missouri River near the mouth of the Kansas River,
where they held a powwow. Illness among the men kept
the party camped there for two weeks. Finally, the Osage
went home. Bourgmont tried to continue the expedition, but
he became ill and had to be carried back to Fort Orleans.
In late September, Bourgmont left the fort again. Finally, on
October 19, 1724, at the Grand Village of the Apaches, near
present-day Ellsworth, Kansas, the French and Indians held a
peace conference. After the Frenchmen presented the Apaches
with many gifts, an agreement was reached. The Apaches
pledged their friendship to the French and guaranteed them
safe passage to Santa Fe. The Osage and other Missouri River
tribes agreed to live in peace with the Apaches, to trade rather
than wage war. Although the French and Indian treaty was
probably an oversimplification of their problems, it was a
monumental feat, bringing together a gathering of more than

The French happily received Bourgmont and the Indian delegation that accompanied him to Paris in 1724. The one Missouri woman who was part of the group returned to Fort Orleans married to a French officer. (Ernest L. Blumenschein, "Return of the French Officer and His Indian Bride to Fort Orleans," mural in the Missouri State Capitol. State Historical Society of Missouri, Columbia.)

two thousand Indians. When Bourgmont returned to Fort Orleans, he asked the fort's chaplain, Father Jean Baptiste Mercier, to celebrate the successful expedition with a special service.

Three weeks later, Bourgmont left for New Orleans and then for France, accompanied by a few representatives chosen by a council of Missouri River Indians. The group received in France by the Duke and Duchess of Bourbon included one young Missouri woman and five chiefs—one each from the Missouri, the Illinois, the Chicago, the Oto, and the Osage tribes. While these Native Americans saw the grand life in France and were entertained by the directors of the Company of the Indies, the peace treaty had not made much of a change in the situation at home.

At Fort Orleans, Father Mercier reported frequent trouble with the Indians. At the request of the Missouri and Osage tribes, Mercier visited their settlements to baptize children and to teach Christianity. The Osage desired to have more missionaries work among them, Mercier wrote. However, he thought that sending missionaries to these Indians was ill-advised, as the fathers would be too exposed to Indian attacks. The French had come to realize that they could never be too certain about their relationship with the Osage or Missouris.

In 1728 or 1729, Fort Orleans began to fall into disrepair. Although Mercier stayed on, the fort was either abandoned or destroyed. With Fort Orleans gone, the trading situation deteriorated. The traders became unruly. Unlicensed dealers attempted to lure tribes into their power. The voyageurs fought and competed with each other, sometimes giving away goods and sometimes making unfair trades with the Indians. The Osage responded with hostility. During the winter of 1733, French Governor Jean-Baptiste Le Moyne de Bienville learned that the Osage had killed eleven voyageurs. He decided he needed to send soldiers into the Osage area to protect the French traders. The Osage, of course, did not like this idea. They denied the eleven killings, admitting only to the murder of one slave and of one engagé, who, according to them, was a tramp. The Osage assured Bienville they had no intention of killing Frenchmen. Their profuse apologies convinced Bienville to drop the matter. The French, Bienville reported to his superiors, certainly did not need to look for new wars.

Although their relationship with the Osage remained shaky, the French were able to accomplish their goal of establishing trade with the Spanish. Beginning in 1739, French traders and Osage traveled together on an expedition to Santa Fe through Apache territory. This Osage-French trading partnership, however, did not prevent further problems between Osage and French traders. In 1740, the Osage killed some

Frenchmen of the Arkansas district. They even took one victim's head into an Indian village.

It seemed necessary to establish a new French fort that would protect voyageurs, keep the traders from competing with each other, and provide fair trade for the Indians. Another fort was finally built. This westernmost of all French forts was chartered in 1744. It was erected opposite Kickapoo Island in present Leavenworth County, Kansas. This post, called Fort Cavagnal, was on high ground overlooking the Missouri River and the Kansa Indian village on Salt Creek. One official trader, Joseph Deruisseau, was granted trading rights on the Missouri River and was given the use of the fort as his headquarters. He was supported there by a commandant and a small garrison. Deruisseau held trading rights from 1745 to 1750 and could and did grant licenses to others to set up minor posts along the river. This plan provided trading control for a short time.

The establishment of Fort Cavagnal did not solve everything, but it did help bring the Kansa, Missouri, and Osage tribes into closer alliance with the French. As a French community grew up around the fort and at other locations along the Missouri River, the Missouri River tribes grew accustomed to the French. Some Indians learned to speak French; some converted to Catholicism; and some even intermarried with the French. The Missouri tribes became French military allies as well. The Osage tribe continued to war against all of its traditional enemies, but they could also be counted on to fight against tribes unfriendly to the French.

During the summer of 1749, rumors of a possible conspiracy against the French arose that involved both the Osage and Missouri tribes. The British, who supposedly instigated the conspiracy, proposed unification of the Missouri River tribes and the Illinois tribes to push the French out of the Louisiana area. The bait to the Indians was cheap British merchandise. The advantage to the British, who controlled the upper Mississippi, was obvious. When the French got wind of this conspiracy idea, they became nervous. They did not know if they could trust the Osage or Missouri. On the other hand, the French should have known by now how difficult it would be to unite the Osage with any other tribes.

That summer three Frenchmen had been killed by the Sioux and one by the Little Osage. The French demanded that the Little Osage turn the murderer over to them. The Little Osage obliged, sending the murderer's scalp to Commandant Jean Baptiste Benoit. However, the Osage later learned that they had executed the brother of the actual killer. The Little Osage then begged the French commandant to come to their village to witness the death of the real murderer.

The Big Osage were equally contrite, perhaps in part because of the hardship they experienced during 1750. While most of the inhabitants of the Big Osage village were away hunting, their longtime enemies, the Panis, attacked. They killed twenty-two Osage, leaving twenty-seven of their own dead. The Grand Osage went to Fort de Chartres to report the death of their chiefs and to ask for French help to avenge their deaths. The French commandant tried to console the Osage with a small gift, but the French would not fight the Osage enemies: they were more and more preoccupied with the approaching war against the British.

When the French and Indian War began on the frontier in 1754 (and in 1756 in Europe, where it was called the Seven Years' War), the French were unable to give adequate attention to the conduct of their affairs in the Missouri River Valley region. The French policy was to promote peace among the tribes and to try to keep them away from English influence. French furriers expected trade to continue with the Indians as it had; and indeed, the fur merchants prospered. However, there were more incidents of Indian hostility. Traders who received their licenses in Canada and had no post in the Louisiana area were often robbed of their goods. Osage parties who found hunters intruding on their land would take the hunters' weapons, clothing, furs, and sometimes their scalps to use as trophies or for their own mourning ceremonies. Although these repeated violent acts by the Osage frustrated the French, the only way to retaliate was to deny them trade. Not only did the Osage object to this action, but merchants protested. The merchants preferred to overlook Indian attacks on voyageurs in order to keep the peace and their business. Meanwhile, the Osage had learned to get their way by making great shows of apology. Their weeping and contrition usually helped them regain the trade they had lost.

As the French and Indian War continued, trading conditions along the Missouri River became even more unsettled. Many merchants did not have goods to trade to the Indians. The Osage felt they had the right to take what they wanted from any traders they found with merchandise. Therefore, when the New Orleans firm of Maxent, Laclède, and Company petitioned the director general of Louisiana, Jean Jacques Blaise d'Abbadie, for a trade monopoly in Missouri, he complied.

D'Abbadie apparently granted the company an eight-year trading monopoly without having consulted with anyone. Merchants protested losing the prosperous Osage trade. When news reached France, the government reversed D'Abbadie's agreement, saying it violated established French policy. Meanwhile, Pierre de Laclède Liguest, a company partner, had already loaded pirogues and left New Orleans to find an appropriate place to establish a trading post. After rejecting Ste. Geneviève because of the settlement's potential for flooding, Laclède temporarily housed his wares at Fort de Chartres while searching for a site. He decided on a location on the west bank of the Mississippi several miles south of the mouth of the Missouri River. Here he had some workmen and his stepson, fourteen-year-old Auguste Chouteau, who was to become very important in Osage trade, start building. On February 15, 1764, work began on the town Laclède called St. Louis. This proved to be a good location for what would become a major fur-trading metropolis.

When the French and Indian War finally ended in 1763 with the Treaty of Paris, the French gave up their power over the Louisiana Territory. Spain acquired the formerly French area on the west side of the Mississippi, while the British took possession of the east bank of the Mississippi north of the Ohio River. When they learned of the changes, the Osage and other Missouri River tribes were confused. The situation the Spanish inherited in the Missouri River Valley was far from peaceful.

# 4

# The Spanish Take Over

Although the perfidy of the Osages is well known, it behooves us to observe always with care international law in order to go on teaching them, and above all in order that the cultivated nations never truly say that we have been imprudent or cruel.

—GOVERNOR ESTEBAN MIRO to Ignacio Delino,
February 17, 1791

When the Spanish took over the Louisiana Territory in 1763, they did so with some reluctance. They wanted a buffer zone to protect their possessions in the Southwest and in Florida. However, they had neither the manpower nor the money to govern this large territory. The transfer of power to the Spanish was in name only for some time. Communications were slow, and a newly appointed French director general for Louisiana had already gone to New Orleans. He had not been informed that his territory was now under the rule of Spain. In the absence of any Spanish officials, he remained the officer in charge.

The first Spanish governor of the Louisiana Territory, Antonio de Ulloa, arrived in New Orleans in March of 1766. He refused to take immediate possession of the area, because he did not have the military strength to do so. Instead, Ulloa agreed to work with the French authority. A two-headed government prevailed until the French director, Charles Philippe Aubry, gave up his command in October 1768. Meanwhile, in early 1767 Governor Ulloa began the military reorganization of Louisiana. He intended to establish new regulations for the Indians of the area, to construct two forts at the mouth of the Missouri, and to stop English traders from invading the Louisiana Territory.

Rather than institute the mission–military post system that had been used to dominate and acculturate the tribes in the Southwest, Spain tried to control the Missouri River Indians through the use of licensed traders, as the French had done before them. The Spanish, however, felt that it was essential for trade to be carefully regulated; only people of good character should be allowed to conduct trade. They also believed in a reward system, whereby Spanish officials would distribute flags, medals, and other gifts to loyal Indian chiefs and tribes.

Ulloa planned three centers from which gifts would be distributed and traders would be sent forth. The centers were at St. Louis, where the Big and Little Osage would receive their presents; at the Arkansas Post on the Arkansas River; and at Natchitoches near the Red River in what is now Louisiana. Actually, the trading system's hub remained St. Louis, controlled primarily by the French. Even after the Spanish garrison arrived in St. Louis in 1770, there were never more than a few Spanish military personnel in residence. Over the nearly forty years of Spanish control, the major fur traders were Frenchmen. Of the seventeen principal congés in 1792, fifteen were French; one was Spanish, and one was Spanish-Indian. Almost all of the engagés who actually conducted the trading appeared to be French.

Ulloa did not stay to see his plan implemented. He was ousted in 1768. The next Spanish governor, Luis de Unzaga y Amozaga, found that dealing with the Osage took an infinite amount of patience. With no money to use for military

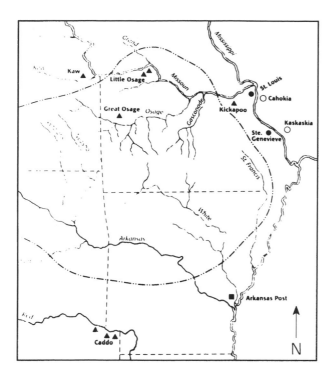

The first Spanish governor of the Louisiana Territory, Antonio de Ulloa, planned two trading centers for the Osage—one for the Arkansas Band at the Arkansas Post and one for the Big Osage and Little Osage at St. Louis. (Map of Tribal Locations in 1775 at the Osage Tribal Museum, Pawhuska, Oklahoma. Photograph by A. E. Schroeder.)

protection, Unzaga had to overlook minor transgressions and to rely on occasional harsh language to try to get the Osage under control. He was baffled, as were all Spanish officials, by the Osages' pledges of loyalty to the Spanish and, at the same time, by their treacherous actions—including robbery and murder. Lieutenant Governor Athanase de Mezières, at the post in Natchitoches, called the Osage the "most . . . deceitful and perverse" of tribes. He felt the only policy they could understand was brute force. Although Unzaga insisted on taking only defensive measures against the Osage, de Mezières provided the Quapaw tribe with bullets, powder, and rewards to bring back Osage scalps. When Unzaga received reassurance from the Osage of their peaceful intentions, he urged de Mezières to call off the Quapaw. However, Quapaw warriors refused to believe that the Osage would keep the peace. The Osage "are not good," said a Quapaw war chief, "nor will they ever be good."

The Osage did not keep the peace. In May 1775, Osage warriors raided the Natchitoches district, killing four Europeans
wintering nearby and stealing horses from a Caddo village.
Despite rebukes, Osage bands also continued their raids along
the Arkansas River. They stripped clean at least three parties
of hunters during the summer of 1776.

Of all the Indian tribes on the Missouri's west bank, the
Big Osage were the most troublesome. The Little Osage and
the Missouri were not innocent bystanders, but their conduct
was not as aggressive as that of the Big Osage. When Unzaga left in 1777, Bernardo de Galvez, the new governor of
Louisiana, continued to try to make peace with the Osage and
to convince them not to commit crimes. Galvez was no more
successful than Unzaga. He did not understand that the Osage
were raised to be warriors and that bravery in battle was a
source of great pride to them. At the time, they had many
opportunities to demonstrate bravery: they were at war with
the Otos, Quapaws, Panis, Panis Piqués, and all the Missouri
River nations. Hunters and voyageurs suffered from Osage
attacks, and colonial settlements were frequently robbed of
horses and supplies.

Yet the Big Osage, numbering some eight hundred warriors
under their principal chief, Clermont, kept the peace with the
traders who were assigned to them. Trade with the Osage was
more profitable than conducting business with any other tribe.
Therefore, the Osage received special treatment. Strict policies
against them were not enforced, because merchants benefited
so greatly from the Osage trade profits.

Spain's attitude toward the Louisiana Territory changed
during the American War of Independence. Both the American
Revolutionaries and the English sought Spain's help. Since
the Spanish thought the Americans were as threatening as
the English, they concentrated their efforts on fortifying their
frontiers against both sides.

The War of Independence ended in 1783. Although the war
itself did not affect the Indian tribes of the Missouri River,
its consequences did. The United States claimed land on the

Residents of early Ste. Geneviève often complained that bands of Osage stole horses and destroyed property. (Mural in the Missouri State Capitol by O. E. Berninghouse, State Historical Society of Missouri, Columbia.)

east bank of the Mississippi down to the thirty-first parallel, midway through present-day Mississippi. Americans argued their right to navigate the Mississippi River to its mouth. The British monopolized trade on the upper Mississippi, and Spain refused to concede its navigational rights on the river. Esteban Miro, who was then governor of the Louisiana Territory, fought desperately to keep the Spanish claims. He hoped to find a route to the western sea and to establish a line of posts from St. Louis westward. This ambitious plan would protect and connect Spain's possessions in North America. Although Miro's grandiose plan was not realized, it did provide incentive to Spanish traders to explore the Missouri River north of the Platte River.

Miro's other ambition was to make peace with the Osage. However, Osage actions made this difficult. The Osage raided and killed in a Peoria Indian village, in Ste. Geneviève, and in hunting camps along the Arkansas River. One particularly brutal incident involved a hunting party. Hunters returned to camp to find it plundered, their large herd of horses stolen, and four people decapitated, including a five-year-old girl. Finally, Governor Miro decided he had had enough. On May 13, 1787,

Miro issued a proclamation declaring the Osage enemies. He wrote:

> Such wicked and barbarous proceedings, contrary to all right and justice, in the midst of my having previously tried on my part all the means of reconciliation, require a vigorous demonstration, not only for the sake of the honor of the Spanish arms, but to give a warning one for all to a nation who are so recklessly breaking the most solemn promises and treaties.

In addition to declaring the Osage to be enemies, Miro prohibited trade with the Osage in Illinois and on the Arkansas River. He hoped to limit Osage trade to Missouri and to induce the Indians to stop raiding and pillaging outside their supposed trading area.

The Osage refused to make amends or to assume responsibility for their actions. Big Osage Chief Jean Lafon said he could not answer for complaints against the Arkansas Osage. Chief Clermont expressed satisfaction that the Arkansas party would be cut from trade. Eventually, however, the trade ban forced Chief Lafon to travel to St. Louis to protest. On October 16, 1787, with several other members of his tribe, Lafon appeared before a council and pronounced:

> It is not I or the young men who are here who have killed; it is some fools over whom I am not master. Do you not have some fools among your young men? These gentlemen who are present here will know that I have done no evil. It is not bravery to die when one is sick, but it is to die fighting. This is the discourse they have told me up to now. This is the word that the rascals make to the chiefs, and which I am reporting. They are stupid.

Lieutenant Governor Francisco Cruzat was not swayed by Lafon's words, nor was his successor, Captain Manuel Perez, who received fifty desperate Osage in St. Louis in the winter of 1788. Perez found the group to be in a pitiable state. Out of fear, he presented them with a few gifts and some food, but he did not give them back their trading rights.

Apparently during 1789 and 1790, the Osage were trading with the English. Although the Spanish restored trade with the Little Osage for a time, the Osages' conduct did not change. Their attacks continued, and in May of 1790 Miro cut off trade with the Osages everywhere in order to "make them listen to reason." Osage pillaging continued with no relief. Meanwhile, St. Louis traders began to complain bitterly. Too many merchants and traders depended on the Indian trade for it to be curtailed. The Big and Little Osage were the most important participants in that trade. Nonetheless, Miro kept the trade embargo in effect. His policy became one of hostility, if not open warfare, toward the Big Osage. His initial hopes for peace with the tribe had proved to be unrealistic. When he retired after ten years as governor of Louisiana, the Osage were still as unruly as ever.

The next Spanish governor of the Louisiana Territory, Francisco Luis Hector, Baron de Carondelet, took office in December of 1791. He had greater problems than any of his predecessors in protecting Louisiana as a Spanish territory. English, French, and American settlers threatened Spanish control. Carondelet attempted to make Louisiana a safer Spanish stronghold by encouraging European settlers to move in and by building up military defenses. He thought he could handle the Osage peacefully. He was disappointed to find that he had to become aggressive. The two-year trade ban, instituted by Miro, had not stopped Osage raids. In early 1792, the Osage killed two hunters on the Arkansas River. Six days later they attacked some Europeans camped on the White River. In March, the Little and Big Osage stole horses and destroyed property in Ste. Geneviève. During that skirmish, the Peoria Indians succeeded in taking an Osage prisoner, either the son or grandson of Chief Clermont. When interrogated, he revealed that two war parties of forty to fifty Osage warriors were out raiding.

By the end of June 1792, Carondelet was ready to destroy the Osage, to "finish with them once and for all." However, a new lieutenant governor for St. Louis, Zenon Trudeau, took over in July. He tried to convince Carondelet that war was not the answer. The first thing Trudeau did was issue an edict establishing free commerce with all Indian nations in Missouri. Trudeau did inform the Osage, however, as previous lieutenant governors had done, that any further atrocities committed by them would result in another trade cut-off.

The Big Osage continued their pattern of raiding, mutilating, and killing in Arkansas. The Little Osage continued stealing horses and destroying property in the Ste. Geneviève area. Finally, Carondelet again ordered trade halted with both the Big and Little Osage. He also suggested to Trudeau that he should encourage any subject "white or red" to "overrun the Big and Little Osages, kill them and destroy their families, as they are disturbers of the prosperity of all the nations."

Loss of trade and the prospect of war caused 120 Big and Little Osage, including 31 chiefs, to pay a call on Lieutenant Governor Trudeau in the summer of 1793. The Big Osage swore they had never stolen a horse or spilled a drop of blood. One chief declared, "It is true that on the Arkansas River some men were murdered and various ones taken prisoner and robbed, but what nation doesn't have its delinquents?" Everything could not be blamed on these so-called delinquents, but this part of the Osage denial had some basis of truth. One band of Big Osage was responsible for most of the crimes along the Arkansas River. Trudeau's response to the Osage dramatics was calm. He told them that Governor Carondelet was very angry and demanded that the Osage improve their behavior.

Although at times the Spanish thought the one solution to the Osage problem might be to kill them all, it was not a reasonable course of action. A Christian nation could not deliberately set out to murder a people, and killing off the Osage undoubtedly would produce new problems. Just the threat of war against the Osage had caused settlers to worry about their safety. If all the Osage turned against the Spanish, it would endanger all Europeans, traders, hunters, and settlers throughout the Louisiana Territory. By invading and trying to wipe out the Big Osage village, as Carondelet had originally proposed, the Spanish might drive other tribes to side with the Osage. The annoying and damaging Osage attacks could easily become a full-scale Spanish-Indian war. Plus, if the Osage were wiped out, their loss of trade would be significant.

French traders Auguste and Pierre Chouteau provided an alternative to annihilation. In March 1792 the Big Osage chiefs gave Pierre Chouteau land near their village to use as a trading post. The land grant treaty, which was signed by one Little Osage and several Big Osage chiefs, declared:

> Brother: as thou hast, since a long time, fed our wives and children, and thou hast always been good to us and thou hast always assisted us with thy advice, we have listened with pleasure to thy words, therefore, take thou on the Rivière a la Mine the quantity of land which may suit thee and anywhere thou pleasest.

In the fall of 1793, the Chouteau brothers proposed constructing a fort on this land near the Big Osage village. The Chouteaus offered to pay for all the expenses of the fort in exchange for a six-year trade monopoly with the Osage. In April 1794, Auguste Chouteau traveled to New Orleans with an Osage delegation to plead his case before Governor Carondelet. Chouteau informed Carondelet that the Osage were continuing to trade despite restrictions. Some furs were traded in St. Louis in the dead of night, but the majority of the Osage fur trade had gone to the English, robbing the Spanish of profitable business. Also, because the Osage had been forced to trade outside their trading area, they were causing trouble wherever they went. Chouteau's proposal not only would keep the Spanish from having to deal with the unruly Osage but also would cost them very little. Pierre Chouteau, whom the tribe both feared and respected, would be the fort's commandant, and the Spanish would be responsible for paying only

Auguste Chouteau, stepson of Pierre de Laclède Liguest, was employed by the fur trading firm of Maxent, Laclede, and Company. Laclède put him in charge of constructing the first buildings in St. Louis in 1764, when he was fourteen years old. Chouteau later became a successful trader and businessman. (Missouri Historical Society, St. Louis.)

for guns and ammunition. These arguments and Trudeau's support convinced Carondelet to allow the Chouteaus to build a fort and have a trading monopoly. While the Osage delegation was in New Orleans, Carondelet, following Trudeau's recommendations, put on a fine show of military strength and presented medals and gifts to Big Osage Chiefs Lafon, Cheveux Blancs, Petit Oiseau, and La Roble Tolle as well as to Little Osage Chiefs La Vente and Le Soldat Du Chene.

The new peace with the Osage had a seemingly shaky start: On the way home from New Orleans, five Osage grew bored with the boat and decided to walk along the river's bank. A band of Chickasaws shot at the unarmed men and killed Chief Lafon and two Little Osage. Amazingly enough, this incident did not prove to cause trouble. Between 1794 and 1797 the Osage problem became practically nonexistent. The relative peace enjoyed in upper Louisiana was largely due to Pierre Chouteau's influence and to Fort Carondelet, which the Chouteaus had named for the governor.

Fur trader Pierre Chouteau, with his brother Auguste, constructed a trading fort near the Big Osage village, creating relative peace between the Osage and settlers from 1794 to 1797. (Library of Congress, *Dictionary of American Portraits*. State Historical Society of Missouri, Columbia.)

However, peace did not last. The Osage were not totally restrained. In late 1797, the commandant at Ste. Geneviève complained of Osage roaming around his district, stealing horses and terrorizing lead miners. Another Osage band robbed several hunting parties along the Arkansas River. In December, a group of Osage fought some Choctaws in the Arkansas River Valley. In January 1798, there were reports of Osages molesting settlers in Illinois. Additional raids occurred in March. More horse stealing, looting, and killing occurred throughout 1798. It appeared that Fort Carondelet was losing its value as a deterrent to Osage crime. Auguste Chouteau lamented that he could not be responsible for Osage behavior:

> This is a nation which will cause trouble for a long time because it is so brutal and so far away from the point of civilization at which they might be made into honest men, that one can hope for this change in them only through the passage of time.

The Osage, however, had lost their goodwill for a number of reasons. There was more than one incident of Comanches raiding Osage camps, killing men and women and capturing children. The Osage were also aggravated by an increasing number of settlers and displaced Indian tribes intruding on their land. Moreover, the Osage claimed that virtually all the tribes in Missouri were united against them, impeding their ability to hunt safely and provide trade furs for the Chouteaus.

In the last year of their trading monopoly, the Chouteau brothers asked the governor to pay for salaries of twenty militiamen at the fort.

> All the profits I've been able to reap have been swallowed up in the foundations of the fort which I have constructed in the midst of this barbarous nation at the risk of my life and of my brother's; for of all the nations which surround us, I scarcely know one more barbarous than the Osage nation and which is more distant from civilization and more unmanageable. It is only by dint of presents and by exhaustion itself that one succeeds with them. Rigor, far from softening them, renders them more ferocious.

Despite the "barbarism" of the Osage, the Chouteaus wished to retain their monopoly of the Osage trade and to attempt to gain back the money they had sunk into the fort. As the last year of their trade agreement ended in 1800, Auguste Chouteau traveled to New Orleans to ask Governor Caso Calvo for an extension. Calvo granted the Chouteaus a four-year license, because he felt they were "worthy of it."

The extension of the Chouteau monopoly agreement produced jealous complaints from at least one St. Louis merchant. At this time the Osage trade amounted to more than half of the St. Louis Indian commerce. Without taking into account the expenses and hardships the Chouteaus had incurred, it seemed the brothers had an unfair advantage. Manuel Lisa, the St. Louis merchant who protested, persuaded other congés to sign a petition demanding that the government cancel the Chouteau monopoly and institute free trade.

The Spanish government took a long time making a decision, but finally, in 1802, it canceled the Chouteau trade agreement and granted the Lisa petitioners the right to the Osage business. After the withdrawal of Chouteau's garrison that fall, the new congés would be responsible for paying the salaries of militia men at the fort and for all other aspects of running the Osage trade. As it turned out, Lisa succeeded in destroying the Chouteau monopoly, but he did not succeed in living up to his obligations. Because of legal and financial problems, Lisa never took over Fort Carondelet. When Chouteau moved out, the fort was quickly ransacked by Big and Little Osage warriors.

Meanwhile, a division occurred in the Big Osage tribe. Before Lisa obtained Osage trading rights in 1802, a faction of the Big Osage decided they were tired of the peaceful ways of the Missouri Osage. This group, which came to be called the Arkansas Osage, moved to the vicinity of the Three Forks of the Arkansas River, where they continued the raids, robberies, and murders that had plagued the Spanish government for so long. Chouteau followed, or as some suggest, instigated the Arkansas Osage. There, while he waited for the outcome of legal actions he had taken against Lisa and the Spanish government, Chouteau traded with the Arkansas faction.

Big Osage chiefs Belle Oiseau and Cheveux Blancs appealed to the Spanish government to do something to bring the two factions of their tribe back together. Even if they had tried, it is doubtful that Spanish officials could have done anything to reunite the two Big Osage bands. The Osage tribe had grown so large and so powerful during the Spanish regime that a break in the unity of the tribe was almost inevitable. The chiefs and the warriors had become more influential than the Little Old Men, and the traditional ways of the tribe had been weakened by European contact and dispute. Incredible changes had taken place, but events that were happening in Europe would cause even more changes in the Osage way of life in the early years of the nineteenth century.

# 5

# The Louisiana Purchase and the Osage World

The Osage discovered after 1804 that the world as they knew it was rapidly disintegrating.

—WILLARD H. ROLLINGS,
*The Osage*

On October 1, 1800, Spain ceded the Louisiana Territory back to France. "Louisiana costs us more than it is worth," Spain's minister of foreign affairs, Mariana Luis de Urquigo, had written in early 1800. Although the land provided Spain with a barrier to protect its other possessions in North America, the cost was too great. Spain spent money for the defense and administration of the Louisiana Territory, and Spanish governors were subject to constant friction with the British, Americans, and French, as well as the Indians. Invasion always seemed possible, and the Osage forays were more than a nuisance.

Spain assumed that if they ceded the Louisiana Territory to France, the French would protect the interior of the North American continent from British and American intrusions.

In fact, they thought they had a promise from the French to occupy Louisiana. In this, the Spanish were very disappointed. Even before the French repossessed their former colony, Napoleon sold the Louisiana Territory to the United States. The territory was formally transferred from Spain to France on November 30, 1803, and then by France to the United States on December 20, 1803.

The purchase of the Louisiana Territory proved to be a very important acquisition for the United States. When President Thomas Jefferson took office in 1801, one of his primary goals was western expansion, but he could not have foreseen the extent of population growth and westward movement during his administration. Nothing contributed more to this expansion than the purchase of the Louisiana Territory, which effectively doubled the size of the United States. The vast area bought from France for fifteen million dollars stretched from the mouth of the Mississippi to Canada and west from the Mississippi to the Rocky Mountains.

The Louisiana Purchase came about because of willing buyers and willing sellers. Jefferson had sent James Monroe to France in 1803 to assist Robert R. Livingston, the U.S. minister in Paris. Jefferson instructed Monroe to negotiate commercial rights in New Orleans. "There is on the globe one single spot, the possessor of which is our natural and habitual enemy," Jefferson said. "It is New Orleans, through which the produce of three-eighths of our territory must pass to market." Included in the products that went through New Orleans were most of the furs from the Osage trade. Therefore, when the right to deposit U.S. goods for reshipment from New Orleans was suddenly revoked in 1802, fur traders had no place to deposit their goods. Although Jefferson told Monroe to secure New Orleans for American trade, he actually hoped to buy the port.

Jefferson authorized Monroe to offer the French ten million dollars for the Isle of Orleans, on which New Orleans sat, and the Floridas (which belonged to Spain, but which Jefferson mistakenly thought were French). By the time Monroe arrived in Paris on April 12, 1803, Livingston had paved the way for the United States to purchase much more than the port. In his talks with Charles Maurice de Talleyrand, the French minister of the Public Treasury, Livingston had advanced the idea of buying the entire Louisiana Territory, which he claimed was of little economic value. Napoleon, seriously in debt and needing funds for his European campaign, had decided to cancel his plans to build a colonial empire in the Americas. The idea of receiving money for land given to him by the Spanish interested him greatly.

On May 2, 1803, the U.S. ministers signed a treaty agreeing to pay the French $11,250,000 for Louisiana and to set aside $3,750,000 for land claims in the territory by French citizens. Although the $15 million purchase price was undoubtedly an incredible bargain (less than three cents an acre!), Monroe worried about exceeding Jefferson's authorization. Also, there were several possible impediments to the treaty. Napoleon's action required the agreement of the French legislature, a technicality he ignored; Jefferson doubted the constitutionality of the purchase, a problem he, too, decided to disregard.

The purchase of Louisiana was by far the most important event of Jefferson's presidency. First, it ended the controversy over control of the Mississippi River. Now the United States could navigate the river without challenge. Second, the purchase opened a huge amount of territory for westward expansion. The population of the United States grew from four million in 1790 to seven million in 1810 to ten million in 1820. People took advantage of the vast expanse of American land and moved west from eastern states. By 1810 the population pattern looked like a triangle with corners in Maine, Georgia, and St. Louis, with settlers spilling into the Louisiana Purchase area.

What about the Native Americans who already occupied the land between the Alleghenies and the Mississippi River? Jefferson assumed that they would continue to move west of the Mississippi to keep from being engulfed by white settlers. Their choices seemed to be to move or to adapt to European ways, give up their vast hunting grounds, and become farmers. Tribes such as the Osage, who already lived west of the Mississippi, would now have to deal with fresh waves of settlers as well as more displaced Native Americans.

The French, Spanish, British, and now the Americans had all hoped to discover a water route to the western sea. Exploration of the area by white men had been constant since the first French explorers had ventured down the Mississippi, but now settlers came in a huge rush. Jefferson could not have anticipated that they would in many cases beat the retreating Indians to the Louisiana Purchase area.

Attempts by native tribes to resist giving up their lands quickly failed. During the presidencies of Jefferson and then Madison, fifty-three treaties for land cession were made by the Indians. By 1815 the Missouri Territory had more than twenty thousand inhabitants. This number did not include the Osage who had lived there when the Europeans came or the displaced eastern tribes who had moved in. The settlement of the Louisiana Territory was sudden, chaotic, and very overwhelming to Missouri tribes.

Long before he became president, Thomas Jefferson had been interested in what lay to the west of the Mississippi River. In 1793, Jefferson and other members of the American Philosophical Society of Philadelphia engaged naturalist André Michaux "to explore the country along the Missouri, and . . . westwardly to the Pacific Ocean." One of Michaux's primary objectives was "to find the shortest and most convenient route of communication between the United States and the Pacific Ocean." Also, Michaux was instructed to gather information on the flora, fauna, and native inhabitants. Michaux never accomplished any of these goals: his journey ended in Kentucky when he was implicated in the efforts of "Citizen Genet" of the French Republic to enlist Americans to fight the Spanish and British. However, scientific exploration of the western half of the continent was realized in the expedition of Lewis and Clark.

President Jefferson had commissioned Meriwether Lewis and William Clark to explore the Louisiana Territory before the Louisiana Purchase had been made. On January 18, 1803,

President Thomas
Jefferson commissioned
his secretary, Meriwether
Lewis, to explore the
Louisiana Territory. (From
*Original Journals of the Lewis and
Clark Expedition*, 1804–1806,
vol. 1, edited by Reuben G.
Thwaites. State Historical
Society of Missouri, Columbia.)

Jefferson sent a confidential message to the U.S. Congress asking for money for an exploring party. He urged Congress to send a group to establish Indian trading houses on the frontier and "to trace the Missouri to its source, to cross the Highlands, and follow the best water communication which offered itself . . . to the Pacific Ocean." Congress approved the proposal and granted twenty-five hundred dollars "for the purpose of extending the external commerce of the United States."

Thomas Jefferson had carefully prepared his secretary, Meriwether Lewis, for just such an undertaking as the exploration of the Louisiana Territory. Although Lewis had never attended college, he had access to Jefferson's large library, and he had developed a deep interest in natural history. Jefferson had never been more than fifty miles west of Monticello, his home in Virginia, but he hoped to guide his twenty-eight-year-old secretary through a trip he wished he could make himself. To get Lewis ready for the journey, Jefferson sent him to Phila-

Lewis chose William Clark as the co-captain for the "Corps of Discovery," later called the Lewis and Clark Expedition. (From *Original Journals of the Lewis and Clark Expedition,* vol. 2, edited by Reuben G. Thwaites. State Historical Society of Missouri, Columbia. Courtesy Independence National Historical Park, Philadelphia.)

delphia to study under botanist Benjamin Smith Barton and astronomer-paleontologist Caspar Wistar. Dr. Benjamin Rush, one of the young nation's leading doctors, prepared a pharmaceutical kit for the explorers and gave Lewis instruction on medical care.

Lewis knew he needed a co-captain for this expedition. He chose his friend, thirty-three-year-old William Clark. Before Lewis became Jefferson's secretary, he had served in the army under General "Mad Anthony" Wayne in Ohio, fighting the Indians in a land dispute. Lewis knew Clark to be an exceptional leader; at one time he had been Lewis's commanding officer. Clark was also an experienced surveyor and woodsman. When he received Lewis's invitation to help lead the "Corps of Discovery," Clark was tending his family farm in Kentucky. He gladly accepted the challenge and assured Lewis that he looked forward to the "dangers, difficulties, and fatigues" of such a journey.

Meriwether Lewis received his official instructions for the

expedition from President Jefferson on June 20, 1803. Although
the Louisiana Purchase agreement had been signed on May 2,
word of the agreement did not arrive from Europe until July.
As far as Jefferson knew, the note he wrote to Lewis was really
a letter of permission to undertake an intelligence mission on
foreign soil. It read:

> To Meriwether Lewis:
>
> The object of your mission is to explore the Missouri River,
> as, by its course and communication with the waters of
> the Pacific Ocean, may offer the most direct and practi-
> cable water-communication across the continent for the
> purpose of commerce.
>
> Beginning at the mouth of the Missouri, you will take
> observations of latitude and longitude, at all remarkable
> points on the river. Your observations are to be taken with
> great pains and accuracy. Several copies of these should
> be made at leisure times.
>
> Objects worthy of notice will be: the soil and face of the
> country, the animals, the mineral productions of every
> kind, and the climate.
>
> You will make yourself acquainted with the names of the
> [Indian] nations and their numbers; the extent of their
> possessions; their relations with other tribes or nations;
> their language and traditions.
>
> In all your intercourse with the natives, treat them in the
> most friendly and conciliatory manner which their own
> conduct will admit. If a superior force should be arrayed
> against your further passage, and inflexibly determined
> to arrest it, you must return. In the loss of yourselves we
> should also lose the information you will have acquired.
> To your own discretion, therefore, must be left the degree
> of danger you may risk, and the point at which you should
> decline; we wish you to err on the side of your safety, and
> to bring back your party safe.
>
> To provide, on the accident of your death, and the con-
> sequent danger to your party, and total failure of the
> enterprise, you are authorized to name the person who
> shall succeed to the command on your decease.

Given under my hand at the City of Washington, this
twentieth day of June, 1803.
Thomas Jefferson
President of the United States of America

Meriwether Lewis spent the spring and summer of 1803 get-
ting ready for the journey. He needed not only to educate himself to fulfill the scientific aspects of his mission—mapping,
identifying plants and animals, taking geological observa-
tions, recording rainfall and weather patterns—but also to
learn as much as he could about the Native Americans of
the region. From Jefferson's letter, it was clear the president
wanted to gain knowledge about the native nations and to
become friendly with them. Part of Lewis's mission was to
search for possible trading house locations and to acquaint
himself with the kinds of trade goods needed to ensure the
friendship of various tribes.

Lewis also busied himself gathering equipment. He pur-
chased more than a ton of supplies, including camping goods,
weapons, scientific instruments, clothing, and research books.
He also ordered gifts to take to the Native American tribes.
Lewis stocked tomahawks and knives as well as decorative
objects—beads, buttons, curtain rings (for ear and finger
adornment), fabric, red paint, and ruffled shirts. The government provided flags, certificates, and peace medals to present
to Indian leaders. The Jefferson Peace and Friendship medal,
which showed Jefferson on one side and the clasped hands of
friendship on the other, was similar to medals that had been
produced for presidents since Washington.

One of Lewis's last jobs was to recruit men to go on the trip.
Six army soldiers, three "on trial" volunteers, and a river pilot
waited with Lewis in Pittsburgh, where the keelboat he had
ordered was being completed. Four hours after it was finished,
Lewis and his men launched the boat. At Louisville, Clark, his
slave York, and more volunteer soldiers boarded to sail on
to a camp near St. Louis, where they would make their final
preparations for the journey.

The explorers set up camp on the Mississippi River eighteen miles from St. Louis and somewhat closer to the mouth of the Missouri River. Lewis and Clark and their entourage spent five months, from December 1803 to May 1804, at the place they called Camp Wood. While Lewis collected the last provisions and packed gifts ready for distribution to the Indians, Clark acted as commander in charge of the men. Pierre and Auguste Chouteau, who both lived in St. Louis when they were not on trading missions, offered their help in finding experienced trapper-traders who knew the Missouri River and the Indian tribes who lived on it. Perhaps the most valuable person who would go on the trip other than Lewis and Clark was George Drouillard, recommended by the Chouteaus. Son of a French-Canadian father and a Shawnee mother, Drouillard would serve as interpreter and chief provisioner on the trip. By the time Clark had assembled the final expedition party, the ten or twelve men originally proposed by Jefferson had grown to more than forty. Besides French rivermen, there were many trained volunteer soldiers.

While the Lewis and Clark party was at Camp Wood, the United States government announced its purchase of the Louisiana Territory. On March 9, 1804, the Louisiana Purchase was celebrated in St. Louis. As government envoys raised the American flag over this little fur-trading town, Meriwether Lewis realized that he was now an official diplomat of the United States. He immediately sent messages to Missouri River Indian tribes informing them that the people of the United States were "their fathers and friends."

When the Osage received the news, they burned the letter and refused to believe it. This reaction may not have surprised Lewis, who had already heard a lot about the Missouri River natives from the Chouteau brothers. The maps and the wealth of information the Chouteaus had about the river and the Indians proved of great value to the two explorers. Of course, they heard many stories about the infamous Osage! Lewis and Clark recognized the prestige and the important location of the

On March 9, 1804, the Louisiana Purchase was celebrated in St. Louis with the raising of the American flag. (Ezra Winter, "The Way Opened to the Pacific," mural in the George Rogers Clark Memorial at Vincennes, Indiana. State Historical Society of Missouri, Columbia.)

Osage nation. They also appreciated the Chouteau family's influence over this powerful tribe.

As Captain Lewis prepared to leave the St. Louis area, he gave his power of attorney to Pierre Chouteau. He also asked Chouteau to escort an Osage delegation to visit President Jefferson. U.S. officials had planned to meet with the Osage even before the Louisiana Purchase had been made. Now that the Osage were on U.S. territory, it seemed extremely important that the federal government develop a good relationship with them.

Both the Osage bound for Washington, D.C., and the Lewis and Clark expedition prepared to embark in May of 1804. The Corps of Discovery left Camp Wood on May 14 in their keelboat and two pirogues. The explorers traveled for only two days. They docked at St. Charles to wait for Meriwether Lewis, who was still making last-minute arrangements for

The Spanish Government House in St. Louis became an American building in 1804 after a brief French occupation. (Missouri Historical Society, St. Louis.)

Pierre Chouteau's party to depart for Washington. Lewis had prepared two boxes of artifacts, which he asked Chouteau to deliver to Jefferson. The boxes included maps, plant and animal specimens (including a live horned toad), and Indian vocabularies. Once Chouteau and his group of Osage chiefs were prepared to leave, Captain Lewis went on to St. Charles, where he found his party had apparently been having far too much fun during its five-day stay. However, the expedition got underway the following day, May 21, 1804.

The Lewis and Clark expedition soon discovered how difficult the Missouri River was to navigate. Their heavy loads caused the keelboat to catch on sandbars, snags, and logs. The men had to pole hard to get upriver. Mosquitoes, ticks, and all kinds of other insects bothered the men. By June 23, 1804, the explorers estimated they had traveled about three hundred river miles from St. Louis. That night they camped on a little island across from a steep bluff on the south side of the river. William Clark noted in his journal that the high bluff across from their camp would make an excellent site for an Indian trading house. He and Lewis decided to mark this point for the first post west of the Mississippi River, and Clark marked the spot "Fort Point" on his map. Eventually, Fort Osage would be built at this location.

Meanwhile, in July, as the Lewis and Clark expedition progressed up the Missouri River, Chouteau and the Osage chiefs arrived in Washington. President Jefferson and Secretary of War Henry Dearborn met with the Osage delegation. They assured the Osage of their friendship. There was no talk of land cession; Jefferson and Dearborn said they planned to keep the Louisiana Territory as an Indian preserve. In fact, Secretary Dearborn promised the Osage that

> All lands belonging to you, lying within the territory of the United States, shall be and remain the property of your nation, unless you shall voluntarily relinquish or dispose of the same. And all persons citizens of the United States are hereby strictly forbidden to disturb you or your nation in the quiet possession of said lands.

Trying to win the Osage trust, Jefferson asked the chiefs what the U.S. government could do for them. Chief Cheveux Blancs told Jefferson that their biggest problem was the division within the Big Osage tribe: two years before, he said, four hundred warriors and their families—around one thousand Osage—had left their native land on the Osage River and moved to Arkansas. Cheveux Blancs said they needed help to bring their tribe back together. Jefferson assured the chief that the U.S. government wanted the Osage to live in peace and harmony and that his representatives would do what they could to help reunite their tribe.

Reuniting the Osage was just one of the jobs given to Pierre Chouteau when President Jefferson appointed him Indian agent for the tribes of Upper Louisiana. Besides trying to heal

The Lewis and Clark expedition left its first stop, St. Charles, Missouri, on May 21, 1804. (Painting by Charles Morganthaler, State Historical Society of Missouri, Columbia. Courtesy St. Charles County Historical Society.)

the breach in the Big Osage nation, Jefferson's government hoped that the Osage and other tribes could be converted into farmers. Jefferson told Chouteau to furnish the Osage with "ploughs, hoes, axes, spinning wheels, looms, and other necessary materials" to help them change their Indian way of life. Not recognizing that the Osage were a seminomadic, hunting, and warring nation, Jefferson thought they could become peaceful and "civilized."

The Osage could not be transformed by a visit to Washington, D.C., or by the distribution of domestic equipment. They continued to act as they had under French and then Spanish rulers; U.S. officials reacted as previous governments had to the Osage mischief. Repeatedly, the Osage raided white communities, stealing and destroying property. Settlers demanded that the Osage offenders be punished and made to pay for damaged goods. In one case a warrior was arrested and would have received corporeal punishment if Chouteau had not intervened. He wrote Secretary of War Dearborn and explained that the Osage did not understand white laws. If

On June 1, 1804, Lewis and Clark noted the mouth of the Osage River. (Mural by Victor Higgins in the Missouri State Capitol. State Historical Society of Missouri, Columbia.)

the warrior had been hurt, he and his tribe would have sought revenge, possibly against totally innocent citizens. The warrior was released. Like the Spanish before them, the U.S. officials talked about peace and friendship with the Osage and put up with their many aggressive acts.

Meanwhile, the Osage continued to have both external and internal problems of their own. Other Upper Louisiana Territory tribes had begun to cooperate with each other. With their common hatred of the Osage, they threatened to war on the Osage nation. Internally, the Osage tribe remained fragmented. The Arkansas faction of the Big Osage, under Chief Grande Piste, refused to listen to Cheveux Blancs's plea to rejoin the tribe. Cheveux Blancs consulted with Chouteau on ways to get Grande Piste's group back into the fold. They decided the only thing that might work would be to deprive the Arkansas Osage of trade. Pierre Chouteau went along with this idea, even though his brother Auguste traded at Grande Piste's village. Chouteau wrote to Jefferson in November 1804 to suggest that "the deprivation of merchandise would be the most prompt means and at the same time the most certain means of reuniting this part of the nation to the total mass." However, depriving the Arkansas Osage of trade was difficult, if not impossible, to supervise.

By the following spring, nothing had happened to bring the two Big Osage groups together. Chouteau again recommended keeping traders away from Grande Piste. Then in June of 1806, Chouteau suggested that a delegation of Arkansas Osage chiefs visit Washington so that President Jefferson could address them directly. After the first group of Osage had gone to Washington with Chouteau in 1804, two other Osage delegations had visited Jefferson. In early 1806, the Little Osage, along with representatives of the Kansa, Oto, Pani, Iowa, and Sioux tribes, had met with the president. In the spring another group of Big Osage went to Washington. Grande Piste's band was the only group of Osage that had not talked with Jefferson.

Jefferson agreed to meet with the Arkansas band. In the fall of 1806, Chouteau went to Grande Piste's village and convinced six chiefs to go to Washington. Grande Piste was dying, but his son, also called Grande Piste, accompanied the group. On December 31, President Jefferson addressed these powerful and independent Osage warriors. His theme was again one of peace and friendship. He urged the Big Osage to solve their family quarrel. "Both parties are my children," he told them, "and I wish equally well to both, but it would give me a great pleasure if they could again reunite; because a nation, while it holds together, is strong against its enemies, but, breaking into parts, it is easily destroyed." The president's talk with the Arkansas Big Osage accomplished little.

Meanwhile, problems between the Osage and other Indian tribes in Upper Louisiana continued to arise. Not only were great numbers of displaced tribes coming into the territory but also almost every tribe was at war with the Osage. The situation was complicated by Chouteau, who wanted to remain friends with the Osage but also was expected to deal with the other tribes. If the Osage trusted him, other tribes did not.

In March 1807, Chouteau's job description changed. He became the Indian agent for the Big and Little Osage, while

William Clark, who with Lewis had recently returned from his expedition, became the Indian agent for other Upper Louisiana tribes and assumed the title of Superintendent of Indian Affairs. At the same time, Jefferson appointed Meriwether Lewis governor of the Territory of Louisiana. The three men— Chouteau, Clark, and Lewis—tried to enforce the federal government's policies to promote free trade with all tribes and to encourage the Indians to adopt a settled lifestyle. Since the Osage were not willing to become farmers, the U.S. government's approach did not work any better than the previous Spanish or French policies.

President Jefferson decided to change course.

# 6

# Fort Osage: Gateway to the American West

If we use forbearance, and open commerce . . . they
[the Indians] will come to us. . . . The factories proposed on the Missouri . . . will have more effect than
as many armies. It is on their interests that we must
rely for their friendship, and not their fears.

—President Thomas Jefferson, 1803

During 1808 the U.S. government began to make
changes in its policy toward the Osage. These changes
reflected a new attitude toward Osage raids, a desire
to regulate Indian trade, and the decision to purchase land
from the Osage tribe.

The first policy change was made in answer to American
settlers in Missouri territory, who demanded that the government do something to protect them from Osage raids. Acting
Governor Frederick Bates thought the Osage should be punished like any other offenders for breaking the law, without
concern that war might result. Bates described the problems
the Osage created:

> About a week ago they . . . loaded the horses which they stole whereever they could find them with the property of the frontier inhabitants. There was no personal violence offered; but the most wanton waste committed on property of every description. Furniture was split to pieces with their Tomahawks; feather beds ript open and destroyed, and every thing which could not be carried away rendered useless to the owners.

President Jefferson agreed that the settlers needed to be protected. He decided that the century-long policy by the French, Spanish, and U.S. governments of avoiding trouble with the Osage was not serving its purpose. Because every government had feared retaliation from the Osage, the Osage had suffered virtually no punishment for their raids. Jefferson felt that all attempts at peaceful coexistence with the Osage had failed. Besides, the U.S. government's friendship with the Osage was presently hurting its relationship with other tribes in Upper Louisiana. Almost all of the other tribes, including the Choctaws, Quapaws, Otos, and Kickapoos, were at war with the Osage. Jefferson determined to try a tougher approach.

When Jefferson appointed his old friend and Corps of Discovery hero, Meriwether Lewis, to be governor of the Louisiana Territory, he told him to crack down on the Osage. Lewis arrived in St. Louis in March 1808. One of his first acts was to ask Pierre Chouteau, Osage agent, to deliver letters to Grande Piste the younger and Cheveux Blancs, informing them of his appointment and of his policy. In his letters or "speeches," Lewis told Grande Piste that if his band did not rejoin Cheveux Blancs's group, the Arkansas Osage would have their trade goods cut off. To make his point even stronger, Lewis painted a picture of Grande Piste's village with no guns or powder or merchandise, a village so vulnerable that enemies "will make cruel war upon you and will carry off your women and children as slaves." Governor Lewis informed the Osage that they were responsible for their actions and demanded that they return stolen property and horses. Finally, because of their past crimes, the Osage were declared "outside of the U.S. government's protection." Therefore, if other tribes wanted to make war on the Osage, Lewis said, they could do so at will.

The second major policy change came in the establishment of both a fort and a factory, or trading post, near the Osage villages. Back in January 1803, Jefferson had received permission from Congress to build Indian trading houses on the frontier. He had planned for twenty-eight posts. The original idea of the trading posts was to provide Indians with a place they could depend on to trade their furs. They would know they could get the merchandise they wanted at the posts at cost. One of the reasons for the trading posts was to lessen the intense competition of traders and provide fair trade for the Indians. Another purpose was to win the friendship of the native tribes. The boundaries of the Louisiana Territory were relatively undefined. The British and their trading companies were encroaching from the north, and the Spanish were still strong in the Southwest. The U.S. government thought it could win the allegiance of the Indians by offering them trade goods at lower costs than the British or Spanish or any of the private traders. The friendship of the natives was important to the safety of Americans settling the Louisiana Territory.

In June 1804, Lewis and Clark had marked the spot for the first U.S. trading house west of the Mississippi. Jefferson approved the intended site, and in 1808 the government decided to start building the trading post. However, U.S. officials determined that there should be not only a factory but also a fort. The Osage were told that the intended fort would protect them from enemy tribes if they chose to live near it, but the fort also served notice that this was U.S. territory. The fort's garrison of troops would be there to control the Osage, Kansas, and Iowas, if the need arose.

On August 7, 1808, Captain Eli Clemson and a company of eighty-one men embarked on the mission to build a fort for the Osage. They left from Fort Bellefontaine, which had been established in 1805 eight miles from St. Louis. The location

FORT OSAGE-1808-JACKSON COUNTY

In 1808, President Jefferson approved the site Lewis and Clark had chosen for the first trading house west of the Mississippi, and Fort Osage was built. (Mural by William Knox in the Missouri State Capitol. State Historical Society of Missouri, Columbia. Courtesy Hammond and Irwin, Jefferson City, Missouri.)

of Fort Bellefontaine had proved to be too far away from the Indian tribes the government wanted to reach. Clemson and his company traveled on six keelboats, which held most of what they would need to set up the trading post–fort at the place Clark called Fort Point. Four of the keelboats held twenty thousand dollars worth of goods that George C. Sibley, the head of the trading post, would trade to the Indians. One of the boats held the army supplies, and the sixth boat carried the food staples for the military personnel.

Besides the river brigade, William Clark asked for and received volunteer military help for the expedition. Eighty members of the St. Charles dragoons, commanded by Clark and guided by Nathan Boone, youngest son of Daniel Boone, set out cross-country from St. Charles on August 25, 1808. In ten days they were building a bridge at Fire Prairie Creek, preparing to cross over to the point on which they would construct the trading house–fort. The next morning, Sunday, September 4, Clark's group arrived at Fire Prairie, which supposedly got its name when several Indians were trapped there and burned in a prairie fire.

Clark's company was met there by a messenger from Captain Clemson. He guided them to join the rest of the company, who had just arrived after a twenty-six-day river trip. They all camped in the Bad Luck Hills near the big eddy of the Missouri River where they were to build. Clark rose early the following morning to check the site he had chosen four years earlier. He "found the River could be completely defended and [the] Situation [was] elegant, this Situation I had examined in the year 1804 and was delighted with it and am equally so now." Therefore, Clark ordered the boats to be unloaded and the work to begin.

Although the company had few sharp axes and many of the men were suffering from dysentery, good progress was made on the fort. By Friday of the week they arrived, two of the planned five blockhouses were finished up to the second floor. By Sunday they were ready for the roofs. One blockhouse was completely finished, two were ready for shingles, and one was almost finished. The last one was well started by the next Thursday when Clark prepared to lead the dragoons back home.

The same day Clark had ordered the soldiers to begin work on the fort, he had sent Nathan Boone and an interpreter, Paul Loese, to the Osage villages to tell them of his arrival at Fire Prairie and of his intention to build a fort there. He also wanted the Osage to know that if they wanted the U.S. government to provide them protection, they would have to move their villages near the fort. Since Meriwether Lewis had informed both the Osage and the Kansas that other tribes could war on them, it was important that they heed Clark's invitation. By the Monday when only two blockhouses were complete, the Osage had begun to arrive. In the first group were two great chiefs and seventy-five followers; they brought word that all the villages were on the move with everything they possessed.

Within two days after the Osage set up camp near Fort Point, Clark made a treaty with them. This treaty represented the third and most profound change in U.S. policy toward the Osage tribe. The government had come to realize in the short time since the Louisiana Purchase that this land could not remain an Indian preserve. Settlers and land speculators were pouring into the area, averaging about two thousand a year between 1804 and 1810. If the Osage could be confined to the western part of present-day Missouri, their warriors would find it more difficult to raid the white settlements to the east, and there would be more land for settlers.

In the eyes of many Americans, settlers had every right to build houses and start farms anywhere in the Louisiana Territory. Some members of Congress, too, felt that the Louisiana Purchase was land the U.S. government had already bought; therefore, there was no reason to rebuy it from the Indians. However, Jefferson believed that if U.S. citizens settled on Indian territory, they should make a treaty with the Indians and buy the land from them at a fair and reasonable price. That is what he wanted Clark to do. Besides imposing discipline on the Osage and regulating their trade, the U.S. government now wanted to buy their land, including most of their traditional hunting grounds. This broke the promise made to the Osage in 1804 by Secretary of War Dearborn. The U.S. government would in fact "disturb" the Osage nation and would acquire Osage land, two things Dearborn had said they would never do.

In the treaty Clark drew up, the U.S. government would take possession of all Osage land south of the Missouri River and east of a line drawn south from Fort Point to the Arkansas River. The land to be ceded to the United States included more than half of Missouri and some of Arkansas. The Osages' traditional home at Marais des Cygnes was slightly to the west of the boundary line and therefore would remain in Osage hands. For this land cession, the Big Osage were to receive an annual payment of one thousand dollars; the Little Osage would receive five hundred dollars each year. Of course, any destruction or theft of white property would be deducted from these annuities. The Indians would have the additional benefits of a blacksmith shop, a mill, farm equipment, and the use of the new trading house. The trading post, Clark told the Osage, was a gift to them from the Great White Father in Washington.

Cheveux Blancs from the Great Osage and Little Osage Chief Sans Oreille immediately decided to sign Clark's treaty. They "touched the feather," took the quill, and made a cross mark. The secondary chiefs also touched the feather and signed. Thus, on September 14, 1808, the first treaty buying land from Indians in the Louisiana Territory was completed. Four cannons were fired, and Clark surprised the principal chiefs by giving them each a gun and gun powder plus $317.74. Clark also distributed tobacco, blankets, and paint to the Osage, whose ceremonies for the occasion lasted all night.

Sans Oreille was especially touched by Clark's gifts. He called Clark his white brother and told him that his "friendship goes to our hearts. We would like to adopt you." Clark hesitated. Although he was honored to be asked to become an Indian brother, he also knew the Osage adoption ceremony was a test of strength and courage. He didn't know how much strength he could muster. He was very weak from both dysentery and the stress of the past days. Sans Oreille understood Clark's concerns and told him he had already proved his courage and strength during the negotiations. The ceremony was short and painless. Clark was christened "Chief Red Hair" and was adopted into the Osage tribe.

Besides honoring Clark, the adoption ceremony gained Sans Oreille considerable influence and prestige. It was common practice for a European who wanted to trade with a tribe to be adopted by an important tribe member, who then took credit for any trading that occurred. With Clark as his brother, Sans

Oreille would be considered responsible for the annuities and gifts Clark distributed to the Osage, a healthy situation for both Clark and Sans Oreille.

However, the treaty that Clark negotiated with the Osage was never ratified by Congress. The Arkansas Osage declared the September treaty to be invalid since they had not been a party to it. Other members of the Big and Little Osage tribes, who had been represented at the treaty signing, complained that the interpreter had not told them they were signing away their lands.

Instead of insisting on the treaty, Governor Meriwether Lewis asked Pierre Chouteau to go back to Fort Clark and demand that all the Osage sign a new treaty. This time, Lewis personally drew up the terms. There was to be no doubt as to what the Osage were signing. There were to be no options. The Osage would simply have the choice of signing or not signing. By not signing, they would be denied trade goods, and would risk war with the government. Chouteau was to insist on the treaty and inform the Osage that

> If they are to be considered our friends and allies, they must sign that instrument, conform to its stipulations, and establish their permanent villages, near the fort erected a little above Fire Prairie. Those who neglect to do so, either themselves, or by the head of their family, must not, under any pretense whatever, be supplied with merchandise, either from the Factory or by individual traders. . . . you will give to each chief warrior, or man of consideration, who signs the treaty, a certificate stating that he has done so, and recommending him to the friendly offices of the citizens of the United States. On these Certificates alone, will the Indians bearing them, and their families, be suffered to trade at the fort.

Chouteau did as he was told. He went to Fort Clark and met with Great and Little Osage chiefs. He read the terms of the new treaty, which were somewhat harsher than the first had been. In addition to the land the Osage had agreed to cede

CHOUTEAU'S TREATY WITH THE OSAGES

Pierre Chouteau went to Fort Osage in November of 1808 and demanded that the Osage sign a treaty with the U.S. government. (Mural by Walter Ufer in the Missouri State Capitol. State Historical Society of Missouri, Columbia.)

to the United States in the treaty made with Chief Red Hair, the new treaty called for the Osage to give up claims on all land east of the line drawn from the fort south to the Arkansas River, including the Osage hunting grounds north of the Missouri River. By this treaty, the Osage would be "ceding and relinquishing for ever to the United States" their land, leaving them with only a narrow strip on the western edge of what is present-day Missouri. Within this narrow area, the Osage would keep possession of their Marais des Cygnes homesite. For this land cession, the United States government agreed to pay the Big Osage one thousand dollars in merchandise and eight hundred dollars annually; the Little Osage would receive half these amounts. Again, the government would provide a mill, a blacksmith, and farm equipment, hoping once more that the Osage would become farmers and renounce their nomadic and warlike customs.

There was no doubt that the Osage understood the consequences of this treaty. After hearing the terms, Little and Big

Cheveux Blancs was the first of the Big Osage to sign the November 10, 1808, treaty. (Painting of "Payouska, Chief of the Great Osages," by Charles B. T. F. Saint-Memin. New-York Historical Society.)

Osage gathered in small groups to talk. Threatening sounds came from some tribesmen; others bowed their heads. Supposedly, Sans Oreille was the one who convinced the chiefs and warriors to accept the treaty. "My children," he addressed them sadly, "the Great White Father has spoken through his messenger, the trader Chouteau. The Great White Father is strong. We are weak. We have no choice but to accept."

On November 10, 1808, the Osage chiefs and warriors touched the feather and signed the second treaty. First to sign for the Great Osage was Cheveux Blancs. Nicheumanee (Walking Rain) was the first Little Osage chief to touch the feather. Chouteau and Captain Clemson signed for the U.S. government, and Clemson ordered that a cannon be fired to

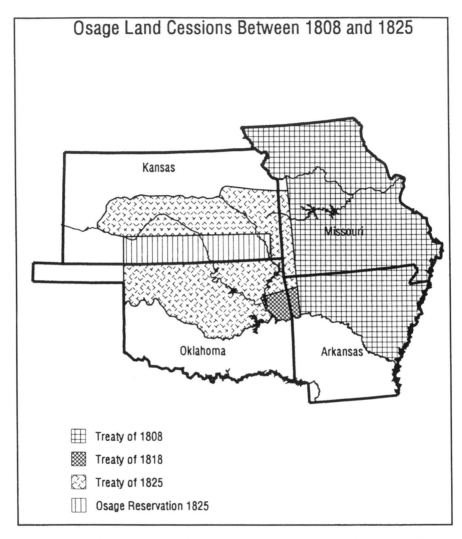

## Osage Land Cessions Between 1808 and 1825

Kansas

Missouri

Oklahoma      Arkansas

     Treaty of 1808
     Treaty of 1818
     Treaty of 1825
     Osage Reservation 1825

The Treaty of 1808 was the first of several treaties that forced the Osage to give up their land. In the treaty of June 2, 1825, the Osage ceded land in Missouri and the Arkansas Territory, giving up their traditional hunting grounds and moving to a reservation in Indian Territory. (Tracey Burnett, Geographic Information Systems, Lincoln University, based on a map by Gary Tong from *The Osage*, Chelsea House Publishers.)

As they were pushed farther westward, the Osage tried to maintain their traditions. Holding the ceremonial peace pipe and rattle, an Osage calls on the Great Spirit to bring peace, happiness, and safety to his tribe. (From Francis La Flesche, *War Ceremony and Peace Ceremony of the Osage Indians*, Smithsonian Institution, Bureau of American Ethnology, Bulletin 101, 1939.)

mark the event. The fort, which was now completed, was officially christened Fort Osage. In St. Louis on August 31, 1809, the Arkansas Osage had the treaty explained to them by Governor Meriwether Lewis. Chiefs Clermont and Cashesegra signed. This treaty was ratified by Congress.

The Osage treaty marked an important turning point between whites and the Osage. For years France, then Spain, and finally the United States had tried to control Osage behavior and trade. None of their efforts had succeeded. Never before, however, had the government attempted to acquire Osage land. For the first time, restraints on the Osage became real. The U.S. government imposed its will on the Osage. From 1808 on, the Osage would be caught in a vicious circle. The only way they could obtain the goods they wanted was to trade furs and skins at the factory. With their hunting grounds so restricted, it became more difficult for them to find enough animals to kill for their hides. Meanwhile, Osage warriors continued to steal horses and commit other crimes to show their bravery, as tradition dictated. Now, American settlers demanded payment for the Osages' destruction and thefts. The government held these claims against the Osage and made the Indians pay at the trading post. If they could not pay, they were forced to cede more land to the United States. There was no way the Osage could continue their traditional way of life, caught as they were in a rapidly changing world.

# 7

# Factory and Fort

Ever since I set foot on this ground I have been busily engaged with Indians; deputations from various Tribes have been here to see our establishment, and to give assurance of their friendly intentions towards the U. States.

—GEORGE SIBLEY, December 13, 1808,
in a letter to his brother, Samuel Hopkins Sibley

The Osage initially rejoiced at the idea of a trading post, and even at moving their villages near the fort for protection. However, shortly after Fort Osage opened, they began to wonder why they had celebrated the opening of the factory-fort. As it turned out, Fort Osage did not really serve the purposes intended by either the U.S. government or the Osage.

The short history of Fort Osage had two phases. The first began with the fort's christening on November 10, 1808, and lasted until June 1813, when the War of 1812 made it necessary to transfer the troops at the fort elsewhere. The second phase was from 1815, when the fort and trading post were reopened, until 1822, when Fort Osage was closed.

The trading post was run by George C. Sibley, Fort Osage's first and only factor, or merchant. Born in Massachusetts, Sibley was raised in North Carolina, where he attended school and served as an apprentice to a Fayetteville merchant. Sibley joined the Indian service in 1805. For two years he served as assistant factor at Fort Bellefontaine, near St. Louis. An organized and fastidious man who always dressed stylishly, he seemed an unlikely person to want to manage a store on the edge of the frontier. Sibley, however, planned to fulfill his obligation to the Osage to the letter.

He received his instructions for running the factory from John Mason, the superintendent of Indian Trade in Washington, D.C. "The principal object of the government in these establishments," Sibley learned in his directions, was "to secure the friendship of the Indians in our country in a way the most beneficial to them and the most effectual & economical to the United States." Sibley was told that his factory should not sell spirits or imperfect goods. Only Indians, not white settlers, could be served. The factory would be provided with a guard from the adjoining garrison. Once a year Sibley would have to send Mason an order for the following year's goods; all bills, accounts, and notes would be sent directly to the Indian Trade department.

A few days after William Clark left the fort in September 1808, the rest of the Osage arrived and set up villages nearby. The Little Osage camped on the riverbank and the Big Osage on the hilltop, as was their custom. Sibley opened the factory right away. From the very first day, he ran a brisk trading business. He noted in his diary that problems with the Indians were few. One of his first concerns was whether or not to let an old Osage buy some blue cloth on credit for his wife's burial. He did.

Sibley's first major problem came in October of 1808. The Kansa tribe—one thousand members strong—had arrived at Fort Osage. Sibley kept up a brisk trade with them from October 12 to October 16, but then cut them off because of their conduct. There were seemingly no repercussions. In December

George C. Sibley was Fort
Osage's first and only
factor. (Oil painting
photographed by Piaget,
Lindenwood College.)

1808, Sibley wrote his brother that many tribes had visited the
factory. "I have done a great deal of trading with them," he
reported in his letter, "and have no doubt of the Success of the
establishment, so I look with certainty for an increase of salary
in the spring."

Perhaps Sibley was due a salary increase that spring, but
instead he received a new Indian agent. Dr. John H. Robinson was hired to come from St. Louis to act as Fort Osage's
medical doctor. However, when he arrived he found that the
fort's Indian agent wanted to leave. Reuben Lewis, Meriwether
Lewis's younger brother, had served as Fort Osage Indian
agent, a subagent to Pierre Chouteau. He quickly tired of the
job, and Dr. Robinson became the Indian subagent to replace
Lewis. Robinson proved to be a good companion for Sibley.
Even after Dr. Robinson's wife and family arrived, the two
men continued to share their meals and conversation.

Dr. Robinson, undoubtedly, had many good tales to tell.
He had been a member of Zebulon Pike's 1806 expedition to

Santa Fe. He was captured by the Spanish and had spent some time in a jail in Chihuahua, Mexico, but he had managed to bring back good maps of the Southwest. Robinson's stories whetted Sibley's appetite for travel to Santa Fe, a trip he would eventually be able to make. Meanwhile, Robinson and Sibley made a strong team. Together they and Captain Clemson tried to run the factory and keep the Osage happy.

Sibley and Robinson got along famously, but the same could not be said for Sibley and Clemson. As is typical in many government operations, tension arose between the civil and military officers at Fort Osage. Clemson and Sibley had totally different outlooks. To begin with, Clemson was suspicious of anyone who dressed in silk vests and stylish cutaway coats, who kept a servant, and who had to have breakfast at exactly 9 A.M. Sibley, who was only slightly concerned about having thousands of Indians camped within yards of the fort-factory, did not allow the Indians to upset his daily routine. Captain Clemson, on the other hand, found the close presence of so many Osage, Kansa, Iowa, Oto, and Missouri Indians to be not only unsettling, but alarming. Of course, he was responsible for the security of the fort and the factory, and he had to deal with any aggression on the part of the Indians.

The first major disagreement between Sibley and Clemson came about because of the success of the factory. A larger and permanent factory building was needed. Since the soldiers had finished the blockhouses and palisades for the fort over the winter of 1808–1809, Sibley asked Captain Clemson if he could use the soldiers to build a new factory. Sibley offered to pay them, but Clemson did not want his men to work on a nonmilitary task. Sibley was so irritated by Clemson's response that he wrote to Superintendent Mason. Mason sent Captain Clemson orders to put his men to work on the factory at once. By spring, when Robinson arrived, forty-two soldiers were working on the new factory, but the relationship between Clemson and Sibley had grown worse.

Sibley and Robinson had to make many decisions on Indian policy themselves, since it took so long to receive directions

When the factory at Fort Osage opened, trade with the Indians was brisk. (From John R. Musick, *Stories of Missouri*, 1897. State Historical Society of Missouri, Columbia.)

from the Washington office. The decisions they made were supposed to be enforced by Clemson's garrison. Yet because Clemson and Sibley were unable to communicate, the civil authority never knew what the military authority was doing, and vice versa. During the summer of 1809, Sibley decided not to trade with two Osage chiefs and about a hundred of their followers; since Clemson knew nothing about this plan, he could not enforce it. In the fall of 1809, an incident occurred that brought the feud between the two men to a climax.

One evening in October, two boats commanded by Joseph Robidoux and François Dorion docked at Fort Osage. Some of the Indians began to cause a disturbance at the landing. According to the interpreter at the fort, the Osage were upset because they thought the traders were going upstream to trade guns and other goods to their enemies. Supposedly, Sibley and Robinson had promised the Osage that the government would not allow any more gun trade upriver. The arrival of Robidoux and Dorion looked like a breach of that promise.

Sibley and Robinson heard the uproar at the dock and went down to calm the Indians. They urged two of the Osage leaders, Traveling Rain and Big Soldier, to tell their people to return to their lodges. Then Sibley and Robinson went back to the fort. As they were standing talking with interpreter George Lorr outside blockhouse number five, Sans Oreille appeared. The Little Osage chief wanted to warn the civil officers that the Osage were about to start a fight. Sibley was alarmed. He told Sans Oreille to go down and tell the Osage that if they molested the boats or the traders, the factory would be closed to them. This threat worked, and the night passed peacefully.

The next day, however, was another story. The two boats left Fort Osage in the early morning, but they did not get very far upriver before grounding on a sandbar. A band of Osage, led by Big Soldier, was waiting either to attack or to help. No one was sure of their intentions. There was a scuffle, and one Osage was hurt. The entire band left to collect weapons to attack the traders, but just about that time Dr. Robinson appeared and successfully broke up the fight. Later both Robinson and Sibley met with Big Soldier and the others who were involved. They scolded them for their actions and told them that for the time being they could not trade at the factory.

What Captain Clemson was doing during this incident seems unclear. On the second day of the confrontation between the French traders and the Osage, after the situation had calmed down, Robinson told Clemson he was surprised that the garrison had not helped control the Indians. Clemson responded, "Such affairs are common and of no consequence." To this remark, Sibley made a fiery retort, one he would later regret. Clemson was obviously nursing several grievances against Sibley besides this latest. Eventually, a year and a half later, Captain Clemson wrote to the secretary of war. He

Joseph Robidoux commanded one of the boats that docked at Fort Osage in the fall of 1809. Robidoux later founded St. Joseph, Missouri. (From *History of Northwest Missouri*, vol. 1. State Historical Society of Missouri, Columbia.)

accused Sibley of causing violence among the Osage, citing this incident as a prime example. Sibley answered Clemson's charges in person. He traveled to Washington and appeared before President James Madison and General John Mason. They sent him back to his post. Sibley felt redeemed by the "increased confidence of the President and Gen'l Mason: the exertion of my enemies to injure me notwithstanding."

The diary and letters of George Sibley show that Fort Osage bustled with activity, not only because of trade with the Indians at the factory but also because of the many travelers and settlers who visited the fort. Besides traders, including members of the Astor Company, scientific expeditions passed through. There were also new people who decided to settle around Fort Osage.

In 1810, a Risdon H. Price of St. Louis arrived with 180 hogs. He and Dr. Robinson started a pork business to supply the military garrison. Ira Cottle and his family came with 110 head of cattle, hoping to sell beef to the soldiers. The Cottles also started a candle business, employing Osage women. They used Sibley's kitchen for melting buffalo tallow to use for both soap and candles. Sibley sent several boxes of their candles to Superintendent John Mason, who thought that the candles might sell profitably in St. Louis but remarked, "They were no great proofs of skill." He hoped that the Osage candle makers might "become more neat in execution" in the future.

With all the travelers coming to and from Fort Osage, George Sibley decided that he wanted to take an expedition to explore the area around the fort. His goals were to visit the villages of the Big and Little Osage, the Kansa, and the Pawnee. Not only was Sibley curious about their villages, but he also wanted to remind the Indians that the factory was there to serve them. On May 11, 1811, he left the fort with interpreter George Lorr and James Henderson, who would take care of the horses. Sans Oreille, the chief of the Little Osage, agreed to accompany his friend Sibley. Two Osage warriors, Little Fire and Cow Tail, acted as scouts and hunters, and two other Osage went along because they wanted to return to their villages. The party was gone for two months. During that time, Sibley saw much of interest to him and kept a journal of his findings.

Sibley, perhaps more than anyone, had come to know and appreciate the Osage. He learned that the women preferred blue or scarlet cloth for skirts; they desired to adorn themselves with tattoos, beads, paint, and mirrors. Sibley became familiar with the Osage habit of pursing their lips at something they wanted rather than pointing to it. To them pointing was more than just rude; it was a death curse. Sibley knew that the Osage believed that whistling attracted ghosts. The quickest way to shoo the Osage away was to whistle. Sibley also could distinguish, and even looked forward to, the Osage morning chant, a howling sound that sometimes alarmed the fort's visitors.

Therefore, Sibley was very disappointed when he realized that the Osage were not happy at the fort. Having visited their home villages, he also understood why. As early as the fall of

1809, the Osage had started returning to their traditional home at Marais des Cygnes. Their migration homeward continued over the next year. By the end of 1810, all of the Big Osage and about half of the Little Osage had left. Fur trader Pierre Chouteau may have encouraged the departure of the Osage from the fort; he told them that wherever they went, traders would come to them. However, the Osage were dissatisfied with the location of the trading post, and they did not like having to live near the fort. One of the reasons was that their lodges there on the Missouri River were too close to their enemies. Rather than offer them protection, the fort actually showed exactly where the Osage were.

March of 1811 found the Osage and Iowa at war with each other. The soldiers from the garrison at the fort were as helpful as they could be to the Osage. They offered to ferry an Osage war party across the Missouri River for the purpose of attacking the Iowa. The warriors returned happily with eight scalps. In May, however, the Iowa retaliated. They hung around the fort, frightening women and children. They stole horses that belonged to the Osage and to the garrison. On the night of May 6, 1811, three strange Indians, presumably Iowa, approached the camp. They refused to halt when asked to do so. A sentry fired at one of the strangers, injuring him. According to Sibley's diary, the shot incited the Osage, who advanced on the stranger and "instantly fell upon him with tomahawks and knives, and in two minutes time cut the poor creature in 50 to 100 pieces. Men, women, and boys engaged in this horrid butchery; and so quickly was it done, that the victim must have felt every blow and cut. His head, arms, hands, legs, feet, fingers, toes, ears, etc., were severed from the body, and the entrails let out." Later that evening, a Little Osage chief burst into Sibley's room holding the head of the slain Indian in one hand and a torch in the other. Sibley dressed and accompanied the chief to their camp, where he tried to calm the Little Osage.

Peace with the Iowa prevailed for a time, but the Little Osage remained dissatisfied with their home at Fort Osage. They, too, wanted to return to their traditional place at the forks of the Osage River. After a late-summer buffalo hunt, they did not return to the fort. By the spring and summer of 1812, the Osage made only infrequent trips to the post, usually just to pick up their annual payments. One of those trips in April of 1812 was disastrous. A few miles away from the fort, the Osage were attacked. Many of their people were killed, and they lost a great number of their horses and a large part of their goods. The survivors would not start back to their homeland until a guard from the garrison agreed to accompany them. As Captain Clemson commented: "Thus we can with truth affirm that the Osages, for whom the establishment was originally intended, dare not visit it. Of course the object of the establishment is destroyed."

Clemson was correct. Traders had posted themselves near the Grand Osage villages on the Osage River. There was no need for the Osage to travel to the factory. Also, the war with Britain, which had been long expected, seemed imminent. It was dangerous for the Osage to leave their homeland, as the Iowa, Potowatomi, Kickapoo, Sac, Fox, and other tribes had allied themselves with the British and would be delighted to attack the Americans and their Osage friends.

Captain Clemson himself longed to be involved in the war. He appealed to the War Department to close the fort and to send him into battle. "There are no possible advantages accruing to the Indians from this situation as a place of trade, nor to the frontier as a military post as in case of an Indian war," Clemson argued, "[we] beg leave with the most respectful deference to recommend its removal." Clemson concluded that the placement of Fort Osage was "a wild, speculative" idea of the late Governor Lewis, and that the "policy has not had the desired effect is obvious."

Finally, in the spring of 1813, the order came through to close Fort Osage. Clemson wasted no time in leaving the garrison, never to return. George Sibley, however, was furious about the decision. He had met with Osage chiefs, who had agreed to fight alongside the U.S. soldiers to defend the fort.

Sibley believed it was imperative for the United States to stand behind the Osage they had befriended. However, the military authorities thought it best to evacuate the fort and defend the safety of St. Charles and St. Louis.

Once the decision was made to close the fort, Sibley moved most of his trade goods to St. Louis. Then with a partner, John W. Johnson, he set up temporary trading houses at Arrow Rock for the Osage and another at the present-day site of Jefferson City for the friendly Sacs and Osage. He was determined to stay on good terms with the Indians he had served at Fort Osage.

# 8

# Last Days in Missouri

They just keep coming like ants.

—OSAGE ELDER,
quoted in Osage Tribal Museum Exhibit

E ngland and the United States agreed to end the War of
1812 when they signed the Treaty of Ghent on December
24, 1814. George Sibley planned to return to Fort Osage
as soon as the war ended, but reoccupation of the fort was
delayed. The main problem was that the law permitting government trading houses had expired on April 1, 1814. Congress
debated whether or not to introduce a new law. Some legis-
lators who opposed a new bill argued that the trading posts–
forts were not accomplishing their intended goals: to provide
Indians with a place to trade their furs for reasonably priced
merchandise, to win the friendship of the native tribes, and to
protect American settlers. Despite these arguments, a new law
was passed to continue the forts.

A garrison and a factory would return to Fort Osage, but
the law's opponents were correct in assuming that President
Jefferson's intentions would no longer be met, at least at Fort
Osage. Little trading would resume. The factory would not

win Indian friendship. The fort would do little to protect settlers, as they were both too widespread to be effectively protected and too aggressive to need the fort's protection. Also, the Osage did not have the power or reputation they once had possessed. Although the U.S. government would continue to meet their requests over the next few years, the Osage were no longer the proud and fierce tribe that had once been feared and revered by all.

However, when the second trading house law passed on May 6, 1815, George Sibley was waiting patiently in Browns-ville, Pennsylvania, with a load of goods to trade to the Osage. He planned to take the trade items to St. Louis and then on to Fort Osage. Before leaving St. Louis, however, he helped distribute presents to the Indians who had signed the treaty at Portage des Sioux. Ten Big Osage chiefs were among those who had been at the council at Portage des Sioux on September 12, 1815. They had "touched the feather" and agreed to "perpetual peace" between the United States and the Osage.

Sibley also remained in St. Louis long enough to marry a "certain fair one, whose beauty, amiable disposition, and elegant accomplishments would adorn a palace." Sibley had met Mary Smith Easton at a party during his many visits to St. Louis during the war. On August 15, 1815, they were married in the home of the bride's parents.

On October 1, 1815, the Sibleys (or perhaps just George Sibley at this point) left St. Louis on a keelboat, which was packed with trade goods as well as Mary's belongings. She had her saddle horse, her piano with fife and drum attachment, her large library, and some furniture. The Sibleys were prepared to live comfortably in the wilderness. Once at Fort Osage, they moved into a house nearby that they named Fountain Cottage. In a letter to his brother, written in July 1816, Sibley described their living conditions:

> Our quarters are very comfortable. . . . With the aid of very fine gardens, a well stocked Poultry yard and an Ice House, we are enabled to live very well. Mary amuses

Mary Smith Easton married George Sibley on August 15, 1815, and moved to Fort Osage. She became a popular hostess and teacher. (Painting photographed by Piaget, Lindenwood College.)

me and herself every day for an hour or two with her piano, on which she performs extremely well; and she has latterly undertaken to instruct her younger sister Louise (who is with us) on that instrument. You may be sure Mary is a very great favorite among the Indians, indeed they literally idolize her since they have seen her play.

Although Sibley was comfortably settled at the fort with wife, piano, and books, Fort Osage was not as successful as it had been before the war. Trading post activity had dropped off considerably. This was due in part to the Osage preoccupation with defending themselves against other tribes, especially the Cherokee, who had been encouraged to move from their eastern mountain homeland by the U.S. government. The Cherokee had been settled on land in Arkansas the government had obtained by treaty from the Osage in 1808. In 1816 Indian agent William L. Lovely bought a large area in northwestern

Arkansas and northeastern Oklahoma from the Osage for the Cherokee, making friction between the two tribes inevitable.

The factory at Fort Osage did not have the attraction for the Osage that it had back in 1808. Competition had increased from other traders, especially the Chouteaus, who had opened a trading post near the Osage villages. Not only was it inconvenient and dangerous for the Osage to leave their villages to trade at the factory but also there was not a large financial incentive. Goods at Chouteau's post were about the same price as goods at the Fort Osage factory.

Although Captain Clemson did not return to Fort Osage after the war, the garrison was reopened in 1815. Not long after it opened, though, rumors began to circulate that the army planned to abandon the fort. When plans went forward to open three new posts on the Missouri River, Colonel Talbot Chambers informed Sibley that the military planned to evacuate Fort Osage. Sibley wrote to General William Clark, governor of the Missouri Territory, to argue his case for maintaining a garrison. He pointed out that the settlers needed protection from the Indians, and the Indians needed help in defending themselves both from displaced Indian tribes and retaliation from the settlers. It was necessary to have military power present, Sibley stated, just because of the number of Indians around. By July 10, 1819, Sibley realized his argument had produced no results. The army abandoned the post.

Sibley stayed on and continued to operate the factory. However, more changes were to occur. The Osage had signed a new treaty with the U.S. government in the summer of 1818. They had ceded more land to the government and had agreed to stay in their traditional homeland in the Osage River area at Marais des Cygnes. Governor Clark, who had negotiated the treaty, thought this agreement would cut down on intertribal wars. However, as he told the Office of Indian Affairs in Washington, D.C., the government could strengthen its control over the Osage and increase trade with them if they opened a trading factory near the Osage villages.

Sans Oreille and a delegation of Osage went to Washington during the summer of 1820 to plead their case. They wanted a factory near them, as Clark had already stated. The Osage representatives said there was unfair competition for their furs and a lack of good trade items to buy at reasonable rates. They were very inconvenienced by not having a blacksmith, a mill, or a factory nearby. With enemy tribes on all sides, they dared not leave their villages to go to Fort Osage. The secretary of war listened to the Osage and wrote to Governor Clark that "many of their complaints are not without sufficient reason." Apparently, the Osage were convincing in their arguments, for plans for a new factory developed.

During the summer of 1821, a trading house was built near the Osage villages at Marais des Cygnes. George Sibley supervised the construction. On December 9, 1821, Thomas L. McKenney, superintendent of Indian trade, appointed Paul Baillio as the factor for the new Osage post. Baillio, who had been a subfactor at Chickasaw Bluffs, would work under the supervision of George Sibley and operate the new establishment as a subfactory of Fort Osage.

Besides the subfactory, three other developments occurred in 1821 that would ultimately affect Fort Osage and the Osage Indians. First, Missouri was admitted to the Union as a state on August 10, 1821. The census reported 70,652 people in the state of Missouri, not including Indians. Another development was the beginning of a trade route to Santa Fe, with Fort Osage as a starting point. William Becknell and three associates made two trips during 1821, forging their way from the fort to Santa Fe. On his return from the second trading expedition, Becknell reported, "An excellent road may be made from Fort Osage to Santa Fe. Few places would require much labor to make this possible, and a road might be laid out as not to run more than thirty miles over the mountains." It would not be long before such a road would become reality, and it would become much more than a trading route.

The third development in 1821 was the establishment of a mission about eight miles northeast of the Great Osage

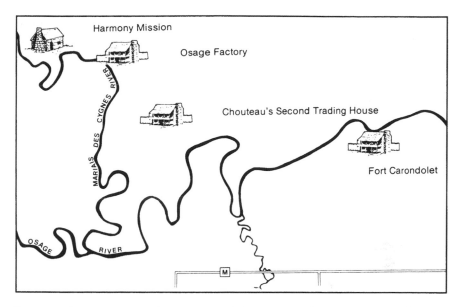

During the summer of 1821, a subfactory to the Fort Osage factory was built near the Osage villages at Marais des Cygnes, and Harmony Mission was established by missionaries sent by the United Foreign Missionary Society of New York. (Drawing at Osage Village State Historic Site, Missouri Department of Natural Resources.)

village. Like the subfactory, the mission that would be built for the Osage received its authorization from the Office of Indian Trade. The Osage delegation that visited Washington in the summer of 1820 asked Superintendent of Indian Affairs McKenney to provide them with not only a trading post but also a school. In 1820 the United Foreign Missionary Society of the East had established Union Mission near Fort Gibson, Oklahoma. It was located just twenty-eight miles from Chief Clermont's Osage village. The Missouri Osage knew of this mission and mission school and believed that the government was favoring the Arkansas band of Osage. They decided they too wanted a school.

Superintendent McKenney and President Monroe were impressed that the Osage delegates asked for Christian education for their people. They felt that a mission among the Osage of

Missouri might do much good. McKenney wrote immediately to the United Foreign Missionary Society in New York City:

> I have had this moment a most interesting interview with the Chief Counsellor and principal warriors of the Osages of the Missouri. The object of their deputation is to solicit the introduction of the school system among their people, and to pray for the means of civilization. I wish I might send you the old chief's talk; but to do so I should have to paint as well as write. He is a most eloquent and able man. I find these Osages are jealous of the Arkansa tribe. They claim to have merited, by holding fast their promises to the government, the first care of this generous sort.

The mission society responded with enthusiasm to the request from Colonel McKenney. Society members sent Reverend Milledoler to Washington as their representative with the full power to secure the necessary legal documents to form an Osage mission. A covenant was made between the Osage and the missionary society. A mission family would embark as soon as possible to the Great Osage Nation with the object "of teaching the Indians the common elements of education and the ordinary mechanic and domestic arts, under the authority and patronage of the United Foreign Missionary Society of New York and with the approbation of the President of the United States." In return for being Christianized and civilized, the Osage agreed to protect the mission family from their enemies, to treat the missionaries with friendship and hospitality, and to give them enough land for the buildings and farms needed.

The board of the mission society hoped to send a mission family to the Osage that same fall. On September 25, 1820, the United Foreign Missionary Society asked for candidates to go to the Great Osage Nation. More than one hundred people applied. By the time the mission society board selected those to go, gathered together necessary supplies, and raised funds for educational purposes, it was nearly spring. Finally, on March 3, 1821, a mission family of twenty-five adults and sixteen children (a much larger group than had gone to Union Mission!) gathered in New York City to prepare for departure. They resolved to found "The Great Osage Mission" at a place to be called "Harmony." They also determined that the children who entered the Harmony school would have Christian names; any person or society to contribute twelve dollars a year for four years "for the Education of a Heathen Child" would "have the privilege of giving that child a name." Although the U.S. government had given the mission family one thousand dollars toward the construction of buildings, additional monies would be needed and collected en route. On March 6, 1821, after receiving final instructions from the mission society board, the Harmony group paraded to the New York City wharf. They boarded the steamboat *Atlanta* and set off at 4 P.M., singing a farewell hymn.

The journals kept by various mission members on the almost two-thousand-mile trip from New York City to the Great Osage Nation read like a complicated and very dangerous board game. For every step forward, there were sacrifices, illnesses, deaths, and then new hopes. Ten families and five single women schoolteachers made up the mission family. Reverend Nathan Dodge was named superintendent. He traveled with his wife and seven children. His assistant was Reverend Bentley Pixley, who came with his wife from Vermont. Leaving New York bound for Philadelphia, the missionaries made many stops to receive contributions of supplies and money for the school at Harmony. At Philadelphia, the group left the *Atlanta* and boarded wagons to proceed to Pittsburgh. From there, they would spend the rest of their trip on keelboats.

On April 19, 1821, the Harmony mission group left Pittsburgh, floating down the Ohio River, holding services and receiving contributions along their route. On April 29 a daughter was born to Samuel Newton and his wife, but by May 5 the baby had died and was buried at Mt. Vernon, Indiana. The next day Sister Newton herself died and was laid to rest in Shawneetown. When the party reached the Mississippi River on May 9, they rejoiced at the idea of having only another six or seven hundred miles to go.

On June 5, the missionaries reached St. Louis. There, according to their journals, they met with Governor William Clark and "the elder and younger Chouteaus, who gave us instructions concerning the Osages." Three days later, they set off again, entering the Missouri River on June 8 and traveling five miles up the muddy river to St. Charles. The last part of the mission family's journey was especially strenuous, as they had to pole their way up the river. They spent three days on a sandbar, but finally reached the mouth of the Osage on June 29. On July 8, another sandbar detained the party. Just when they began to make good progress again, their boatmen decided to go on strike. The cause of this first recorded strike in Missouri was the lack of liquor. The boatmen refused to go on until the missionaries supplied them with spirits from their medical supplies. The Harmony mission family proved it could be more stubborn than the boatmen. They refused the demand and sat for three days until the boatmen decided to go back on duty.

On August 2, 1821, the missionaries passed the mouth of the Little Osage River and laid their eyes "upon the most beautiful prairie." Shortly thereafter, they came to Chouteau's trading post and an Osage village. Although many warriors were absent on a hunt, a number of Osage families came to welcome the missionaries and to help them find a site for their mission. Brothers Dodge, Newton, and Jones decided to advance to the place upriver where Sibley was building his trading factory. Sibley had recommended a site; and when the three men saw it, they agreed that it would be suitable. The Osage promised to give the missionaries whatever land they marked out. On August 13, the site chosen by Sibley was given to the Harmony family by the Osage council. It was an area abundant in timber, surface coal, limestone, and clay. There was a creek and good rich prairie for farming, pasturing, and mowing. Another important attribute of this location was that it was on the wagon route from the new factory to Fort Osage, seventy-eight miles distant.

As the summer drought had caused the Little Osage River to become very shallow, the mission family had to leave their keelboats and carry their supplies overland. By late August they had finished unloading their boats and were lodged in tents at their site on the Marais des Cygnes River about two miles above where that river joined the Marmiton to form the Osage. The location was near present-day Papinsville in Bates County, named for fur trader Melicourt Papin, who had settled there in 1809.

The Osage were helpful and friendly to the newcomers. Mrs. Jones wrote that she and others had visited the Osage "wigwams" and had been given gifts of corn and watermelon. She reported that the Osage "appear fond of our children, often clasp them in their arms, and bring them presents of nuts." Mr. Jones agreed that the Indians seemed happy to have the missionaries there. He called the Osage a noble race. His description of the men matched other descriptions from two hundred years earlier: "The men are large and well built— not many of them are less than six feet in height." The first impressions of all seemed to be that the mission would work. As Jones concluded, "We have great encouragement to believe that it will not be long before their habits will be changed, and they will become both civilized and Christianized."

The general conviction of all the missionaries was that the Osage were in need of civilizing and Christianizing. Reverend Pixley found their situation to be pitiable. He reported to the domestic secretary that the Osage did indeed pray, but their prayer (which began at dawn) was a loud sobbing, crying chant that could be heard more than a mile away. He also found the Osage practice of muddying their heads and faces to be puzzling and certainly dirty. Especially distressing to the missionaries was the Osage habit of wearing little or no clothing. The men would wear only a breechcloth, and the children were naked, even in cold weather. One teacher, Miss

HARMONY MISSION FOR THE OSAGES-1821-BATES COUNTY

The Harmony Mission and the mission school were built on the bank of the Marais des Cygnes River near present-day Papinsville in Bates County. (Mural by William Knox in the Missouri State Capitol. State Historical Society of Missouri, Columbia.)

Comstock, explained her view of the Osage dilemma to her friend in Connecticut: "How frequently do I weep over the moral blindness, and pray that Christians may do much to remove it." Mr. Sprague wrote, "It is painful to reflect on the condition of the Indians to whom we have come. The moon they call heaven, to which we are going at death. The sun they call the Great Spirit, which governs the moon and earth. When asked, 'Where do the bad white men go?' they answer, 'to the moon.' "

Before the missionaries could begin their work of civilizing and Christianizing the Osage, they would be sorely tested. On August 25, just as they were about to begin building the log houses they knew they would need before winter, Brothers Chapman and Fuller arrived from Union Mission. They came to meet the translator from Fort Osage, encourage the

Harmony missionaries, and offer their help. One of the young Harmony teachers, Sister Eliza Howall, immediately fell in love with Brother Fuller. After a five-day courtship, Eliza left as Fuller's bride.

The wedding celebration over, the mission family was ready to get to work when ague, fever, and dysentery struck. By mid-September almost everyone was sick. On September 25, only four men out of sixteen were able to work. Heavy rains set in during October, causing further illnesses and leaving the mission family shaken and unsure. In mid-October Brother Newton was well enough to travel to Fort Osage to get some help. Sibley provided supplies, a boy to cook for the group (as all the women were ill), and some laborers to help build the cabins. In November, Mrs. Montgomery and her newborn died, as did Mrs. Belcher's infant and Mr. Seely. With much help, ten cabins had been built by the end of November. As the remaining missionaries were able to move inside, their health began to return. The cabins, sixteen feet square, were constructed with puncheon floors and log walls. They had good chimneys and were secure enough to keep the missionaries dry and warm.

By January 1822, the Harmony family was ready to start the mission school that they had come to direct. Since they had not built a schoolhouse, they decided to use one of the log houses for a school. The first student was Charlotte Stearnes, a Kansa-Osage, who began on January 11. She was joined on January 14 by Catherine Strong, white and Osage, and Sarah Cochran, French and Osage. Brother Dodge reported to the Domestic Mission secretary that there were twelve students by late January. The children were of both genders and of all sizes. Five were full-blooded Osage, and seven were of mixed ancestry.

The children seemed to be able students. One of Miss Comstock's students, a twelve-year-old daughter of a chief, had learned all of her letters and was writing well after only six days at school. The missionaries were disappointed in the number of students, but the Osage promised them more children would come when they returned from the winter hunt. Chief Cheveux Blancs, however, was more pessimistic, saying he did not think the school could be a success until the meddlesome traders were driven away. Cheveux Blancs and his band had been living on the Neosho River in present-day Kansas since about 1815. Although he returned to set up a village about nine miles from Harmony Mission and sent two of his children to the mission school, he moved back to Neosho after a few months. Dodge admitted in his regular letter to the missionary society that they had found "much difficulty in persuading the natives to give up their children, and in keeping them after they have been given up."

Reverend Dodge decided that his first major task would be to master the Osage language. He wanted to be able to speak with the Indians, but he also hoped to translate Scripture and readers for the students' benefit. Of great help in this endeavor was the Fort Osage factory interpreter, William S. Williams, also known as "Old Bill." Bill helped Montgomery and the other missionaries with the spoken language. "One very favorable circumstance for us," wrote Reverend William Montgomery, "was having quite convenient to us the only competent interpreter in the country." With Old Bill's help, Pixley, Montgomery, and Union Mission Brother W. C. Requa put together a dictionary of the Osage language. The "Osage First Book," a 3½-by-5¾-inch primer, was printed in Boston in June 1822. As the first book ever published in the Osage language, much was expected of this 126-page grammar.

Meanwhile, Old Bill also helped the Harmony family translate Scripture for the purpose of preaching to the Indians. For two years, Bill Williams closely associated himself with the Harmony missionary family. Then their friendship came to an abrupt end. Perhaps the split was caused by the failure of the missionaries to follow Old Bill's advice about a sermon they wanted to preach. Perhaps Bill had grown tired of always being at the missionaries' beck and call. Perhaps he was also fed up with their moralizing.

In any case, one day when Reverend Pixley asked Bill to help him translate the biblical story of Jonah and the whale, Bill refused to do so. He said the allegory was not suitable for a sermon. Contrary to Bill's advice, the minister insisted on preaching it anyway. Pixley should have listened to Old Bill. A whale story would never work in Missouri. At the end of the sermon, one old chief rose. He stated: "We have heard several of the white people talk and lie; we know they will lie, but that is the biggest lie we ever heard." At that, the chief took his people from the church. The Sunday attendance, school attendance, and the missionaries' morale were all affected by this episode. It was also the last time Old Bill made himself available for consultation.

The mission school, however, did continue, and Old Bill's daughter was one of the school's first and longest-attending pupils. Rebecca Williams, Bill's oldest daughter by an Osage woman, was admitted to the mission school on February 12, 1822. In the mission report of 1828, Rebecca had been in the school for six years and was fifteen years old. One of her accomplishments as a student was her superb spinning ability. Under Sister Wooley's tutelage, Rebecca and her half sister, Mary Ludlow, had spun a web of twenty-seven yards of cotton. Mary had been in the school four years in 1828; according to the report, she had become an excellent scholar.

Other students at the school included the daughter of Sans Oreille, who had died. Mrs. Sibley enrolled the little girl in June 1822, but she only stayed a little more than a year. Two of the chiefs who had gone to Washington to petition for the factory and the school, Sans Nerf and Moneypushee, brought children to the school. Moneypushee brought one child. The two children brought by Sans Nerf were his daughter's sons, aged thirteen and seven. The older boy was, as Sibley recorded, "the heir to the throne of the Osage nation." In other words, he was the grandson of the famous Osage chief, Cheveux Blancs, who had died in 1808, and the son of Cheveux Blancs the younger. He would inherit his father's position if he proved deserving.

It is difficult to measure the success of the Harmony Mission school. The students who attended did learn something about whites that would help them cope in future years. They received Christian names, and learned English, domestic skills, dress, and the Christian faith. Since the Osage would never again be able to live in isolation from the white men, perhaps the school, which taught about white ways, was successful.

In terms of numbers of students, the school never grew to be very large. In 1824, there were eighteen pupils; in 1825, thirty-eight; in 1826, twenty-four; in 1830, forty. The enrollment then dwindled until the school was closed in March 1836. The students themselves changed often. Perhaps as few as seven completed their course of education in the basics of reading, writing, math, and domestic arts.

The missionaries admitted that under the best of conditions the educational results were not what they had hoped, and the conditions were rarely at their best. In the first year of operation, things seemed peaceful. However, trouble soon broke out between the Osage and the Cherokees. Despite a treaty with the Cherokee in 1822, the Osage were never at peace with their unwanted neighbors. In 1823, the Creeks and then the Kickapoo encroached on Osage property, causing the Osage to retaliate. The Pawnees stole horses and took Osage prisoners, which led to more fighting.

Besides trouble from Indian tribes, the changes in U.S. government policy toward the Indians caused a constant uproar in the Osage Nation. The Osage found themselves losing all the advantages they thought they would gain when they got their own factory, mission school, mill, and blacksmith. Missouri's statehood in 1821 was the least of the Osages' political problems. As early as June 1821, the long-debated government trading house system seemed likely to collapse. Superintendent of Indian Trade McKenney gave George Sibley permission to travel to Washington to give testimony before the Senate. McKenney assembled data and gathered witnesses to defend the factory system. However, the fiery oratory of Ramsay C. Crooks, fur trader John Jacob Astor, and Missouri Senator

Thomas H. Benton defeated the trading houses. On May 6, 1822, Congress passed a law discontinuing the factories.

Governor William Clark received directions about closing Fort Osage from the Indian office:

> In order to satisfy the Indians and to induce them to give assent freely to this measure, you are authorized to distribute among them, presents, in goods, to such amount as may be necessary . . . taking care to obtain the abrogation on as reasonable terms as possible.

On August 17, 1822, government agent Samuel Blunt arrived at Fort Osage to close the trading post. The Osage chiefs were called together at Marais des Cygnes to receive their gifts and to sign a new treaty. On August 31, 1822, the Osage chiefs, including Cheveux Blancs the younger, made twenty-two marks on the treaty. For a sum of $2,329.40 in merchandise, the Osage gave up the benefits they had received in the treaty of 1808 and the guarantee of a factory at Fort Osage. Almost immediately, Chouteau and other traders persuaded some of the Osage, including Cheveux Blancs's people, to move south away from their Marais des Cygnes homeland, causing further disintegration of the Osage Nation.

At the same time the Osage signed the 1822 treaty, George Sibley and subagents Baillio and Boggs signed an agreement to buy the rest of the Fort Osage trade goods. Since Sibley was the only one with any security, he signed for the seven thousand dollars worth of goods, a debt he would spend the next ten years paying. In 1827 Sibley and his wife left Fountain Cottage to go back to St. Charles. There, to help pay their debt, they would establish a boarding school for girls, now Lindenwood College.

Fort Osage's history ended in 1822. The soldiers were the first to leave. With the treaty of 1822 the traders and Indians departed. By 1823, only the site where the fort stood remained, as settlers had carried away and used logs and beams from the frontier post to build their own houses. Sibley would leave his legacy at the fort, however, for his brother-in-law Archibald Gamble bought the Fort Osage property and laid out a town called Sibley.

The fort, long before it was reconstructed as a historic monument, would remain an important location. Its site would be the gateway to the Santa Fe Trail. When the trail was surveyed in 1825, every mile ticked off coming and going to Santa Fe was measured from Fort Osage. This was not an accident. George C. Sibley of Fort Osage was one of the three commissioners named by President John Quincy Adams on March 16, 1825, to survey the Santa Fe Trail. He would also be the one to negotiate still another treaty with the Osage. On August 10, 1825, the Santa Fe Trail commissioners met the Osage at a place called Council Grove, now a town in Kansas. There, Sibley, Benjamin Reeves, and Thomas Mather signed a treaty with the Osage to gain the right-of-way for the trail through what had become Osage territory. This Council Grove Treaty was the second major treaty with the Osage in 1825.

The first 1825 treaty had spelled the end of the Osage homeland at Marais des Cygnes. Governor Clark said this was the hardest treaty he had ever made, and he feared he might be damned in the hereafter for his part in the agreement. According to the government, the treaty that was signed in St. Louis on June 2, 1825, would offer the Great and Little Osage "that protection of the Government so much desired by them." In return for this "protection," the Osage agreed to cede all their lands in the state of Missouri and in the territory of Arkansas. They were then given the right to occupy for as long as they chose to do so land reserved for them: "Beginning at a point due east of White Hair's village [on the Neosho River in present-day Neosho County] and twenty-five miles west of the western boundary of the State of Missouri, fronting on a north and south line, so as to leave ten miles north and forty miles south of the point of said beginning, and extending west, with the width of fifty miles, to the western boundary of the lands hereby ceded and relinquished by said Tribes or Nations." The treaty was signed by sixty chiefs, chieftains, and warriors of the Great and Little Osage. The Osage delegation received two thousand dollars upon signing and four thousand dollars in merchandise delivered to their villages. The government would pay the tribe seven thousand dollars annually for twenty years, and would furnish them with many head of livestock and provide a blacksmith and houses for four chiefs. The many benefits listed, however, could not justify that the government was forcing the Osage off land that had been promised to them forever.

Witnesses to the treaty included most of the people who had been instrumental in the Osage encounters with traders, trappers, and settlers, including Pierre Chouteau and his son. Governor William Clark's presence was essential. He had the longest-standing relationship with the Osage, and he and the Osage shared a mutual admiration for each other. Even though Clark thought the treaty was a farce, he had finally come to realize that nothing could stand in the way of America's westward expansion, not even a fierce nomadic tribe.

The Osage were pushed to a strip of land fifty miles wide in the southern part of modern Kansas. This would not be the tribe's last move nor its last attempt to try to accommodate the white men. But this move would be the most significant in Osage history. The mighty Osage were forced to give up their traditional homeland at Marais des Cygnes, the final sacrifice of the many other traditions they had given up along the way to becoming "civilized."

# Afterword

# The Osage Retain Their Tribal Identity

It took Father Schoenmakers fifteen years to make a white man out of me, and it will take just fifteen minutes to make an Osage out of myself.

—PAW-NE-NO-PASHE, OSAGE CHIEF, around 1875, from Terry P. Wilson, *The Osage*

The 1825 treaty removed the Osage from Missouri and established them on a reservation in what is now southern Kansas. The land given to them was a strip 50 miles wide and 125 miles long with several square miles on the eastern end designated as an unoccupied buffer zone between Osage Territory and advancing settlers.

For about fifteen years, the Osage lived on this reservation and followed their traditional way of life. Hunting and warfare continued to be the chief occupations of the men. Women raised corn, beans, and squash, and gathered berries, nuts, and other foodstuffs from the forests and prairies. The Osage continued to wear Indian clothing, the men preferring their leggings, breechcloths, and moccasins. The women often chose

cotton dresses but decorated themselves with the silver orna-
mentation they had always favored. The Osage ceremonies, if
anything, became more important to them, as they celebrated
war, peace, and seasonal changes in the traditional ways.

However, change had to come as whites continued their
attempts to "civilize" and Christianize the Osage. The U.S.
government had never given up trying to turn the Osage
into farmers, and an 1839 treaty promised them plows, cattle,
hogs, and other necessities. The Osage resisted farming and
became increasingly dependent on the buffalo for their own
basic needs and as trade goods.

Catholic missionaries came to Osage territory and had a
little more success than the government in altering the Osage
way of life. Father John Schoenmakers founded the Osage
Mission in southeastern Kansas in 1847 and lived among the
Osage until his death in 1883. The Osage revered Schoenmakers, using a variation of his name as their word for priest.
Schoenmakers and other Jesuits converted many mixed-blood
Osage, but most full-blooded Osage refused to become Catholic, just as they refused to become farmers.

During the 1850s, trouble was caused by settlers and other
Indian tribes encroaching on the Osage land. The Osage fought
these trespassers. In 1859 the Osage agent at the Indian Office
tried to help the tribe by bringing in federal troops to evacuate
unauthorized settlers. However, as soon as the troops left, the
non-Osage population returned. These trespassers did not care
that the Kansas reservation had been given to the Osage for
"as long as the grass grows and the water flows." Nor did they
care that the Osage had already given up their homeland in
Missouri. The illegal settlers not only moved onto the Osage
reservation but also stole horses and fields. Some settlers even
moved into Osage cabins while the Indians were buffalo hunting. They also pressured the government to open up this rich
land for white settlement.

The Civil War interrupted the land dispute. Most Osage
did not understand the issues that divided the country; some
fought on one side or the other. After the war, however, the

Father John Schoenmakers
founded the Osage
Mission in Kansas in 1847
and stayed to teach the
Osage until his death.
(Osage Mission, Osage, Kansas.
Jesuit Missouri Province
Archives, St. Louis.)

Osage found that settlers still wanted their reservation land. In 1866, government surveyors quickly divided the Osage property into lots, ready to sell to settlers for $1.25 an acre. And once again the Osage were moved.

A removal treaty was signed in 1870, which relocated the Osage to Indian Territory in what is now the state of Oklahoma, from the ninety-sixth meridian on the east to the Arkansas River on the west. Most of the Osage left their Kansas reservation for the 1870 fall buffalo hunt and then traveled to their new land. Although they were not happy to leave their old reservation, the Osage who did move seemed happy with their new surroundings.

The U.S. government continued to try to "civilize" and Christianize the Osage. Government agents tried to teach the Osage to farm, and Catholic as well as Protestant missionaries hoped to convert them. The Osage became very discontented

Chief Black Dog
(Tschon-Tas-Sab-Bee), one of
the tribal leaders during the
1860s and 1870s, was called a
"blanket Indian" by
government agents, because he
refused to give up his Osage
ways. He is shown with a
tomahawk and pipe. (From
George Catlin, *North American
Indians*. State Historical Society
of Missouri, Columbia.)

as reservation authorities persisted in providing them with
what the white men thought they needed. Allotments of foods
the Osage were unused to eating and boarding schools to
teach their children white men's ways were unacceptable to
Osage traditions. The Osage revolted by setting up their own
constitutional government, which could represent them.

During the 1890s, the U.S. government pressured the Osage
and other tribes in Indian Territory to divide their reservations
into individual allotments. Private ownership would allow the
government to convert this land and the rest of Oklahoma
territory into the state of Oklahoma. The Osage resisted and,
not surprisingly, were the last Indians to give up their reservation. Finally, in 1906 the Osage National Council agreed to
give up common ownership. The council did not make the
decision because of outside pressure but because the Osage
reservation did not have the cultural integrity it once had.

The first tribe to establish their own tribal museum, the Osage proudly display artifacts and documents associated with their history in the Osage Tribal Museum, in Pawhuska, Oklahoma. The city was named for the great Osage chief, Pawhuska, or Cheveux Blancs. (Photograph by A. E. Schroeder.)

There were pockets of Osage who continued to live in the traditional way, but there were also non-Osage and mixed-blooded Osage living in the territory. Individual ownership of land clearly meant the break-up of the Osage way of living, but for all practical purposes that had already happened.

The Osage, however, were left better off financially than any other tribe of Indians. Oil and natural gas had been found on the Osage reservation in 1894, and since 1896 the Osage Nation had been receiving annuities on petroleum produced from reservation wells. When the tribe agreed to individual land ownership in 1906, some provision had to be made for the oil annuities. By an act of Congress, the Osage Allotment Act, all Osages on the tribal membership list as of July 1, 1907, would share in the division of the land and the resources.

Because of their newly found wealth, the Osage had again become a powerful tribe. However, the oil-rich land brought its own set of problems. The Osage continued to have to fight for their rights and for their way of life. The Osage, who are now sometimes identified as the rich Oklahoma Indians, have been more successful than most tribes at maintaining a tribal identity. Although their way of life has been forever changed by encounters with traders, missionaries, settlers, and oil men, the Osage are still proud of their heritage and their history.

# For More Reading

*America the Beautiful: Missouri,* by William R. Sanford and Carl R. Green (Chicago: Children's Press, 1990), describes the natural features of Missouri and has an entire chapter on the first Missourians—the mound builders, the Osage, and European explorers, missionaries, and settlers.

*Before Lewis and Clark: Documents Illustrating the History of Missouri, 1785–1804,* vol. I, edited and with an introductory narrative by A. P. Nasatir (Lincoln: University of Nebraska Press, 1952), contains letters, journals, and other documents written by Spanish and French governors and traders with an interpretative essay by Nasatir.

*The Beginning of the West: Annals of the Kansas Gateway to the American West: 1546–1854,* by Louise Barry (Topeka: Kansas State Historical Society, 1972), provides a year-by-year account of the great westward movement.

*Chez Les Canses: Three Centuries at Kawsmouth: The French Foundations of Metropolitan Kansas City,* by Charles E. Hoffhaus (Kansas City: Lowell Press, 1984), tells of the French discoveries, explorations, and settlements along the Missouri River.

*Fort Osage: Opening of the American West,* by Rhoda Wooldridge (Independence, Mo.: Independence Press, 1983), relates the story of Fort Osage, beginning with President Jefferson's decision to expand government trading posts to serve Native Americans.

*The Imperial Osage: Spanish-Indian Diplomacy in the Mississippi Valley,* by Gilbert C. Din and A. P. Nasatir (Norman: Uni-

111

versity of Oklahoma Press, 1983), is a detailed report of the era of Spanish government of Osage territory.

*The Incredible Journey of Lewis and Clark,* by Rhoda Blumberg (New York: Lothrop, Lee, and Shepard Books, 1987), is an account of the Lewis and Clark expedition, written for young readers and complete with pictures and maps.

*Indians and Archaeology of Missouri, Revised Edition,* by Carl H. Chapman and Eleanor F. Chapman (Columbia: University of Missouri Press, 1983), uses artifacts and line drawings as well as text to trace the history of Native Americans in what is now the state of Missouri.

*The Osage,* by Terry P. Wilson (New York and Philadelphia: Chelsea House Publishers, 1988), is one volume in a series, *The Indians of North America,* written for young people, which describes the problems between American Indians and Europeans from their first encounters to the twentieth century.

*The Osages: Children of the Middle Water,* by John Joseph Mathews (Norman: University of Oklahoma Press, 1961), is a social history of the Osage written by a historian who grew up on an Osage reservation and whose great-grandfather was William Shirley Williams, "Old Bill," the interpreter for the missionaries at Harmony Mission.

For More Information: The Osage Tribal Museum, Library, and Archives, P.O. Box 1359, Pawhuska, Oklahoma, 74056, phone (918) 287–4622.

# Index

# About the Author

Kristie C. Wolferman, a Kansas City historian and teacher, is also the author of *The Nelson-Atkins Museum of Art: Culture Comes to Kansas City* (University of Missouri Press).